# Outside
# Insight

# Outside Insight

## Navigating a World Drowning in Data

JORN LYSEGGEN

PORTFOLIO
PENGUIN

PORTFOLIO PENGUIN

UK | USA | Canada | Ireland | Australia
India | New Zealand | South Africa

Portfolio Penguin is part of the Penguin Random House group of companies
whose addresses can be found at global.penguinrandomhouse.com.

First published 2017
001

Set in 13.5/16 pt Garamond MT Std
Typeset by Jouve (UK), Milton Keynes
Printed in Great Britain by Clays Ltd, St Ives plc

A CIP catalogue record for this book is available from the British Library

Hardback ISBN: 978–0–241–27372–2
Trade Paperback ISBN: 978–0–241–28826–9

www.greenpenguin.co.uk

MIX
Paper from
responsible sources
FSC
www.fsc.org
FSC® C018179

Penguin Random House is committed to a
sustainable future for our business, our readers
and our planet. This book is made from Forest
Stewardship Council® certified paper.

To Kai and Izzy

I won the cosmic lottery when you were born.
I am so proud of you. I love you so much.

# Contents

## Part Three: Outside Insight in Practice

## Part Four: The Future of Outside Insight

# Preface

In the summer of 2001 I took a step back and tried to identify the macro trends that would shape the world in the years to come. I was set on starting a new company and tried to identify an important trend to ride. One trend that I found very intriguing was the explosion of online information. We were drowning in information, and manually it was simply too time-consuming and hard to make sense of it all. The obvious answer to the problem seemed to be a piece of software that could track and analyse all this information automatically.

That is how the company Meltwater was started. We were two guys and a coffee machine, and we started the company in a shack in Oslo, Norway (our address was Shack 15), with starting capital of US$15,000. Our vision was that when executives and decision-makers arrived for work in the morning and had their usual cup of coffee, our software would create a summary of what had happened in the world during the previous twenty-four hours in a form that was so simple to read that within seconds an executive would get the key updates that he or she needed about competitors, key clients and their own brand. Our slogan was 'Informed decisions', because we wanted to help executives to take advantage of the information that was now available online in addition to all the traditional data they had at their disposal.

At the time we did not realize how big a macro trend we had stumbled upon. Initially, we focused on online news and company websites. We didn't anticipate the rise of social media. Facebook was founded in 2004, Twitter in 2006. Blogs didn't reach mainstream attention until around 2007. All this new online content fuelled a need for new, sophisticated software with the ability to analyse billions of documents every day. Today smart algorithms, natural language processing (NLP), machine learning and big-data techniques are used to create analytics and insights from online news and social media that we would not have dreamed of back in 2001.

Over the years Meltwater has grown into a global business serving more than 25,000 corporate clients in more than a hundred countries. Our clients range from medium-size, local companies to large multinationals. In one way or another we serve 50 per cent of the Fortune 500 companies. We serve every industry, and our clients comprise everyone from Coca-Cola to the Vatican. From humble beginnings we have grown to 1,400 employees, with sixty offices in six continents.

From our clients we have learned ingenious ways to use external information. In addition to the obvious uses, such as competitive intelligence, measuring client happiness and product development, we have also come across a range of surprising cases that we hadn't anticipated. The University of Oslo used our service to measure the speed with which a new spelling of the word 'ketchup' in Norwegian was adapted. A ten-person company from southern Sweden selling windows (glass ones – not the Microsoft software) tracked regional news reports for burglaries in order to generate sales leads. A government agency in a European country analysed online chat groups to investigate suspected cases of insider dealing.

Working with clients all over the world and seeing the value they can extract from external information has over the years created a growing realization that we have barely scratched the surface in terms of the role external information will play in decision-making.

Consumers and companies today produce online content at an unprecedented rate. Consumer engagement online and in social media is showing a steady increase. Companies are embracing the internet as a strategic arena to promote their brand, products and jobs, and are increasing their online investment and content creation accordingly. With the rise of new, richer content openly available on the internet, ever more sophisticated business insights can be created.

I believe we are on the cusp of a big transformation when it comes to corporate decision-making. I believe that in the coming years the use of online information will change the way boards are run, the way we develop strategies, the way a company's health is measured and the way executive pay is earned.

These are mind-boggling prospects, and certainly way beyond anything I imagined when I started Meltwater back in 2001. Thanks to the World Wide Web and the rise of social media, the internet has become a treasure trove of consumer insights and competitive intelligence. Today this information is largely underutilized. As companies jockey to improve their positions in an increasingly dynamic and fast-paced competitive environment, the companies with the best ability to anticipate change, and to respond accordingly, will win. Central to this will be a company's ability to use external data and to create insights from the outside.

Jorn Lyseggen
San Francisco, March 2017

# Introduction

On 25 April 2016, VentureBeat, a tech blog that covers the Silicon Valley ecosystem, reported that, in the week leading up to its Q1 financial report, Apple had been cutting all of its contract recruiters.[1] This was taken as an ominous sign, and when Apple's financial figures were reported the next day, they showed a 13 per cent drop in revenue.[2] This was the first quarter in thirteen years that Apple had reported a negative sales development. The market's reaction to the slump was to shave $58 billion off Apple's market value, roughly equivalent to the market value of the German car company BMW.

This book describes the valuable insights that can be found in the information that companies and people leave behind on the internet — our 'digital breadcrumbs' — and how this information is mostly overlooked in corporate decision-making. Job postings, social media, blogs and patent applications are rich sources of forward-looking information. They reveal how much a company is investing, how happy its clients are and its future market positioning. In spite of their obvious strategic value, these sources of information are not commonly utilized today. In this book we will show that those who do pay attention to this new class of data types will develop a superior understanding of their competitive landscape and gain an 'unfair' advantage over their competitors.

## Outside Insight stories

This book tells the stories of many different organizations that are already using Outside Insight to gain a competitive advantage and improve their decision-making.

A special Facebook monitoring unit in the NYPD was able to use Facebook data to trace and convict the murderers of an innocent teenager caught in the crossfire of gang warfare, in a crime with no witnesses.

In its early days YouTube benchmarked its media coverage with that of its competitors to see how successful it was in building its brand and creating a following. Its early lead in media mentions was an early indicator that YouTube would be the winner in the online video space.

The American retailer Racetrac used external data to increase the accuracy of its revenue predictions. By incorporating external leading indicators – data normally not used for budgeting – it was able to reduce prediction errors by 15 per cent.

In just four years the Swedish watchmaker Daniel Wellington grew from nothing to selling more watches than Rolex, using Instagram as the primary marketing channel. Daniel Wellington mobilizes its clients as brand ambassadors and is an example of a new generation of brands that was 'born social' and fully masters the viral potential of today's digital world.

Hike, a home-grown Indian messaging app, was able to overtake Facebook Messenger in less than three years and become the second most popular messaging app in India, beaten only by WhatsApp. Hike's secret weapon is rigorous social media analytics, used to inform its product development. New product features are carefully determined based on consumer preferences found in social media.

EQT, a leading European venture capitalist, is developing a sophisticated data science tool called the Motherbrain to find early-stage companies with traction. This initiative is based on the idea that, as companies grow and become successful, they leave behind online breadcrumbs such as job postings, social media buzz and media coverage. By using sophisticated software to monitor the information that is generated online, EQT hopes that it can find the most promising start-ups in Europe before its competitors.

Social media can also be used to predict elections. In 2016 Meltwater correctly predicted the result of the Brexit referendum and the Trump victory in the US presidential election. Traditional surveys pointed, in both cases, to a different result, but online analysis painted a more accurate picture and showed that Brexit and Trump had dominated support in social media. When the votes were counted, the results were more in line with the social media analysis than with the traditional polls.

## *A new decision paradigm*

Most companies today do not utilize external data in a systematic manner but instead focus their analyses and rigour on internal data such as company financials. The problem with such an approach is that it is very reactive. Internal data is the end-result of historical events. Running a company based on internal data such as last quarter's financials is like driving a car looking in the rear-view mirror.

The main thesis of this book is that decision-making is up for a major overhaul and needs to adjust to a new digital reality. The internet has transformed the way we communicate, get news, shop, socialize, advertise and bank. Yet, despite all these changes, corporate decision-making processes have remained surprisingly static.

In this book a new decision-making paradigm is proposed. It's called Outside Insight (OI), and it is an approach focused on anticipating changes in the competitive landscape by following and analysing the online breadcrumbs that competitors, clients, suppliers and other players in your ecosystem leave behind online.

The new approach to decision-making proposed moves away from the old paradigm centred on inwardly focused Key Performance Indicators (KPIs), financials, annual plans and quarterly reviews. Rigour is instead directed towards real-time analyses of external data. It is an approach that moves the focus away from what *you* are doing to what *the industry* is doing and, crucially, to understanding and anticipating changes in your market conditions in real time.

## A new software category

The need to analyse the plethora of information found online will give rise to an entirely new software category. This new software category will be to external data what business intelligence (BI) is to internal data. In this book this emerging software category is also called Outside Insight (OI).

While BI is primarily focused on company-specific operational metrics, most of which are lagging performance indicators, OI is concerned with a real-time understanding of the ebb and flow of the competitive landscape in order to anticipate future threats and opportunities.

The technical requirements are very different for the two software categories. While BI software is mostly focused on data that is structured in nature, OI software needs to be much more sophisticated and will have to understand text and be able to find patterns in large quantities of unstructured data. For this reason OI relies heavily on techniques from big data, machine learning and predictive analytics.

OI is adding a new level of sophistication to the

executive toolbox. With OI, executives can look beyond a company's data and develop a real-time understanding of how the whole industry is developing. With the help of vast computing powers in the cloud and modern data science techniques, the impact of all external factors can be measured and analysed, bringing Porter's Five Forces to life in dashboards and real-time alerts.

I wrote this book because I believe that Outside Insight will shape the next decades' thinking around company strategy and decision-making. Outside Insight extracts valuable forward-looking insights from a whole range of data sets that are largely ignored today. This data is from a third party and is unaffected by internal biases. It can be used to create an apples-with-apples comparison of you and your competition – in real time. Such an analysis would create a lot of value for boards, executives and operational teams alike.

We are living in a world where we are drowning in data. So far the new data types online have been mostly ignored. We can choose to continue to ignore them and consider them all noise, or we can approach them opportunistically and mine them for new insights. By analysing external information found online we can derive new insights that we cannot find in our internal data. This Outside Insight will help us make better decisions and create more successful strategies. It is my belief that within the next few years most companies will have no choice but to invest in systems and processes to become Outside Insight companies in order to stay relevant.

## *The structure of this book*

Part I of this book, A New Digital Reality, describes how the world has changed and how new data types found on the internet can be mined for forward-looking insights.

Part II, A New Decision Paradigm, discusses how access to real-time information about your industry changes decision-making in three important ways.

Part III, Outside Insight in Practice, offers a simple framework for getting started with Outside Insight today and outlines how to incorporate it into more advanced stages down the road. Part III also includes practical examples of how Outside Insight is used in executive decision-making, in marketing, for product development, for risk detection and in making investment decisions.

Part IV, The Future of Outside Insight, outlines important technical obstacles that need to be solved, what new data types we can expect and what concerns Outside Insight can be expected to raise once it becomes more widespread.

Outside Insight is still in its infancy. We have a lot to learn before we can harvest its full potential. This book contains success stories of innovative companies that are already using Outside Insight to their advantage.

It is my hope that this book will inspire the reader to

take advantage of external data in a more systematic way. It is also my hope that this book can be the first small step in the overhaul of corporate decision-making and start the process of adjusting to a new digital reality.

# Part One

## A New Digital Reality

# Chapter One

## Everyone Leaves Online Breadcrumbs

Owen Mundy, an art professor at Florida State University in Tallahassee, became an internet sensation overnight in July 2014 when he launched a website called 'I Know Where Your Cat Lives', a data experiment pinpointing the location of pet cats all over the world, using metadata unknowingly provided by their owners. Mundy estimates that there are over 15 million images tagged with the word 'cat' shared on Instagram, Flickr and Twitpic currently.[1] But what these photographers don't know is that digital cameras and smartphones embed latitude and longitude coordinates in each image.

Professor Mundy realized that anyone could gain access to the geographic coordinates of the photographs if the users had not protected themselves through the appropriate privacy settings. 'This wasn't just my problem; it was the millions of users of social media who didn't know,' he said. Iknowwhereyourcatlives.com launched with a million cat snaps mapped to within eight metres of their location. It quickly went viral. The site now has 5.3 million photos of cats.

But the owners of the internet's favourite animal are not the only ones leaving digital trails online. We all leave a rich trail of online breadcrumbs as we go about our lives in a digital world. But unlike Hansel and Gretel, we often leave these details unintentionally.

The internet is awash with photographs. Photoworld (part of Europe's largest photo company, CEWE) estimated in June 2015 that 8,796 photos were shared every second on Snapchat.[2] According to the same report, Instagram and Facebook users upload 58 million and 350 million photos every day respectively. Then there's Weibo, WhatsApp, Tumblr, Twitter and a whole host of photo-sharing sites. In 2016, in the highly anticipated annual Internet Trends Report, Silicon Valley venture capitalist Mary Meeker, of Kleiner Perkins, estimated that in 2015 people uploaded an average of 3.25 billion digital images on the internet every day.[3] With an estimated 3 billion people on the internet today, that represents 7.6 photos per person per week.

And it's not just photos. We leave many more digital breadcrumbs out in the open with clues about our lives. When we tweet, we share our location, who we are with and what we are doing. On LinkedIn we list our education and work history. On Facebook we broadcast information about our whereabouts, what music we listen to, which brands we like, which organizations we support, which causes we champion, what and where we like to eat and which future events we plan to attend. Beyond the information that we actively produce and post publicly, our phones are full of apps recording our locations, who we talk to and text, and how we spend our time and money.

Every day we produce 500 million tweets,[4] upload 350 million photos and click 'Like' 5.7 billion times on Facebook,[5] write 100 million blog posts and upload 432,000 hours of video on YouTube.[6] On Twitter and Facebook alone we share twelve items per week. Each of these items is a record in a publicly available journal documenting our whereabouts and what we are up to.

In this chapter we will take a closer look at what insights can be found by analysing the trail of breadcrumbs each and every one of us leaves online.

## NYPD follows the Facebook trail

The wealth of online information that people leave behind has been noticed by the police. Indeed, they are increasingly using digital clues to piece together missing information, using online breadcrumbs as active components in solving crime. Ten years ago detectives would investigate an incident by interviewing witnesses and suspects. But people wouldn't always tell the truth or would struggle to recall with the level of detail required. Today online breadcrumbs can bring to light crucial evidence.

For example, monitoring of Facebook by a special unit of the New York Police Department (NYPD) helped in June 2013 to convict the murderers of Tayshana Murphy, a teenage girl caught up in a dispute between two gangs. There were no witnesses to the event, but the NYPD was nevertheless able to build a strong enough case to convict two gang members, using evidence from online breadcrumbs on Facebook.[7] Ten years ago, without the ability to follow and analyse these online breadcrumbs, the case would have had a very different conclusion.

On the day of the murder two messages were posted on the Facebook account of Carlos Rodriguez, aka 'Loso', who was associated with a rival gang of 3 Staccs, which operated out of Grant Houses, where Murphy lived and was murdered. The first read: 'we had like five brawls in one day and then we left.' Rodriguez's second message stated: 'somebody clapped the chicken girl in the head.' 'Chicken' was Murphy's nickname.

Although the identity of Murphy's killer is still unclear – there were no actual witnesses to the event – two men were convicted of the killing. Tyshawn Brockington, twenty-four, was convicted of second-degree murder in June 2013. Ten months later Robert Cartagena, twenty-three, was convicted of intentional murder.

After Cartagena's conviction, it became clear how significant the monitoring of social media had been to the NYPD investigation. In June 2014 the district attorney for New York County, Cyrus Vance Jr, announced the largest indicted gang case in the history of New York City.[8] In total, the authorities arraigned 103 members of three gangs from the Morningside Heights area. The charges included two homicides, nineteen non-fatal shootings and fifty other incidents involving shootings. All of the defendants were charged with conspiracy to commit gang assault in the first degree, a charge that carries a sentence of five to twenty-five years.

To build their case, investigators and prosecutors had followed the usual procedural investigative routes – the gumshoe work of interviewing witnesses and other sources, monitoring 40,000 phone calls made from correctional facilities, combing through hundreds of hours of CCTV footage and phone records. They had also engaged in a form of police work that is becoming increasingly routine: they had reviewed more than a million social media pages. Facebook was the preferred social network of the gangs – in the indictment, the word 'Facebook' is used 171 times.[9]

## Companies also leave breadcrumbs

Individuals are not the only ones leaving online breadcrumbs. Companies also leave an online trail. As companies invest in new products, launch marketing campaigns, establish partnerships and roll out other initiatives to increase their competitiveness, they leave a trail of online clues about their intentions, freely available for anyone to analyse.

At Meltwater we undertook a small project to investigate what competitive intelligence could be extracted from job postings. We analysed data from all the job postings available on LinkedIn from 15 September to 15 October 2013 for Meltwater and three adjacent companies in our industry: Cision, Vocus and LexisNexis. We broke the data down by location, job type and required experience. It was astonishing to see how much information a simple snapshot of the hiring patterns among the four companies revealed in terms of difference in strategy, operational focus and company DNA.

The first thing that popped out of the data was the difference in rate of growth. Meltwater, Cision and Vocus were all about the same size at the time, but Meltwater had more than twice the number of job openings, indicating a significantly stronger growth rate. Vocus and LexisNexis had similar amounts of openings, indicating that they were growing at similar rates. LexisNexis was about twenty times the size of Meltwater, but had a comparable number of published job postings, indicating a significantly slower growth rate.

Studying the job postings by geography revealed very different market approaches. Cision only hired in the US and was clearly US-centric. Vocus also had most of its job openings in the US but had a few openings in the Philippines. This was a big surprise for us, but later we learned that Vocus offshored some lower-level work to the Philippines to reduce costs. Two-thirds of job openings at LexisNexis were in the US, with the rest in Australia, Canada and Hong Kong – all English-speaking markets. Meltwater had a distinctly different pattern. Our biggest single country of hiring was the US, but otherwise recruitment was very international, with openings across Australia, Canada, China, France, Germany, Hong Kong, Japan, Malaysia, the Netherlands, Singapore and the UK. Looking at the data, Meltwater was clearly more global in its approach than its peers.

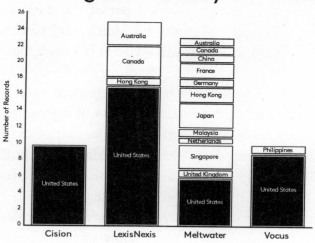

Hiring Patterns by Location

# Hiring Patterns by Job Type

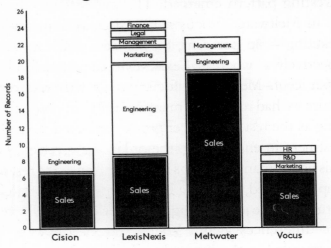

# Hiring Patterns by Experience

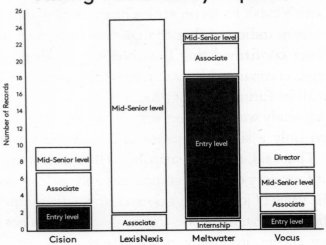

Studying the job postings by job type, a new and interesting pattern emerged. The majority of job openings in Meltwater, Vocus and Cision were in sales and marketing – 80 per cent, 80 per cent and 60 per cent respectively – whereas LexisNexis lagged behind with 44 per cent. Meltwater's focus on growth was evident because we had roughly as many openings in sales and marketing as the rest of the peer group combined. Examining investment in engineering, the order was reversed. LexisNexis had as many openings in engineering as the rest of the group combined, signalling investments in new products.

Studying the job postings by experience level revealed more differences again. Vocus and Cision were both well rounded in the sense that they hired evenly across all experience levels. Meltwater primarily hired entry-level people, whereas LexisNexis recruited almost exclusively at mid- to senior level. Combining the data on LexisNexis's focus on senior hires alongside product investment indicated that changes were on their way. It was later confirmed that LexisNexis was developing a strategic companywide new technology platform powering all its future content products.

This study was based on very limited data and represented only a single snapshot at a particular point in time. That said, this data snapshot tells a fascinating tale about four very different companies and their outlook.

The value of job postings doesn't stop with competitive intelligence. Imagine if you also analysed the job postings of key clients, important vendors and other important stakeholders in your ecosystem. Used in a systematic and rigorous fashion, job posting data can help you understand your competition, which clients you should invest in, which suppliers to choose and which companies to partner with.

## The indiscretion of LinkedIn connections

Another trail of online company breadcrumbs is generated from the connections created on social networks such as LinkedIn and, increasingly, Facebook. If the CEO of your company suddenly establishes a number of relationships on LinkedIn with buy-out firms, don't be surprised if the company is for sale. If the CEO also establishes links with sell-side advisers, the significance could hardly be spelled out more clearly. If the latest relationships come from Goldman Sachs and JP Morgan, it is likely you are preparing for an IPO (Initial Public Offering). New relationships on LinkedIn can represent a chance encounter at a dinner party or signal the early stages of a new client, a new partner or a new employer relationship. If more than one relationship is created with a company, that is a tell-tale sign that this is about more than a chance encounter.

I try to be very careful about how I use social media. For example, recently I was in the process of evaluating whether or not to buy a data science start-up from Uruguay on behalf of Meltwater. A few months previously I connected with the company's founders on LinkedIn – reluctantly at the time, but I thought it was rude not to accept the invitation. We met the company originally in order to evaluate a potential outsourcing job, which in itself was not a hypersensitive issue. However, anyone who discovered this connection and subsequently studied the start-up could see that the company had developed a successful developer community around a data science platform. If this was important enough for key executives of Meltwater to get involved in, it wouldn't be hard to conclude that a data science developer community was a potentially important strategic roadmap for Meltwater.

Once we got to know this company better, we concluded that we wanted to explore a full acquisition of the company instead. As part of the due-diligence process I travelled to Montevideo, a good sixteen-hour journey from San Francisco, to visit the thirty-strong team. During my travels I was careful not to post my location on Twitter or Facebook. There were several group photos taken during my stay, but none was posted on social media. Before and after the trip I was cautious when speaking about it, and I was deliberately vague about my exact whereabouts and what I was up to.

## The tales of a company's website

The corporate website is an obvious place to look for clues about what is happening inside a company. There you can read about big client wins, awards and other significant accomplishments. Similarly, any changes to the executive team will be covered and fleshed out on the page containing management bios.

Companies use their website to share all the latest positive updates with their clients. In the process they are also inadvertently broadcasting that information to competitors and suppliers.

When Meltwater launched in 2001, one of the great selling points of our service was that we could notify you of changes to any web page. This was a very simple service, but it turned out that our clients loved it and used it to track their competitors with a lot more rigour than they had previously done. Using this service, they would be notified immediately if a competitor issued a press release, changed the prices of their products or launched a new sales campaign.

The messaging on a company's website is carefully crafted by communication professionals. Studying what is being said and not being said can tell you a lot about a company's market positioning and strategic intention.

Let us take a look at the front pages of the websites of four of the biggest tech companies in the world today and study how they position themselves.

In August 2016 Apple smears a photo of its newest iPhone across the whole page. There is no doubt about what they are pushing. Apple is, today more than ever, first and foremost the company behind the iPhone.

The message on the HP website is: 'The 3D printing

revolution starts now.' HP positions itself as an innovative future-oriented company, building on its legacy as the world's leading printer company.

IBM has a more complicated message: 'IBM X-force, changing the way to act and share on global threat intelligence.' Their positioning seems to be around intelligence and offering their clever algorithms to solve your problems.

Microsoft surprisingly sports a shining new computer on their website. Their message is simply 'Introducing Surface Book'. The world's largest software company is clearly keen to break away from its traditional software revenue. With Surface Book it is signalling its intention to fight it out with the Mac and iPad.

Companies put a lot of effort into crafting the messaging and communication on their website. Carefully analysing the changing content on your competitors' websites will give you a lot of valuable competitive intelligence.

## The social media buzz

As social media moved from obscure guest pages in the mid-1990s to increasingly popular online social hubs a decade later, companies suddenly lost control of the communication around their brands and services. With the rise of services such as Twitter, Facebook and LinkedIn, a new reality was born in which a single client could set the agenda while the whole world was sitting ringside watching how the company handled itself.

A company's website reveals how a company wants to be perceived by the rest of the world. Through social media you can tune in directly to the voice of a company's clients. Through social media you can get a real-time insight into how well a company is doing in terms of product, customer support and general customer satisfaction. The example below shows customer satisfaction over time for Tesla benchmarked with its peer group, consisting of Mercedes, BMW and Audi. Customer satisfaction is measured as a function of the sentiment on the respective companies' Facebook pages. Interestingly, in spite of all its media coverage, Tesla has been lagging when it comes to the happiness of its customers. The trend, however, is very positive, and by Q2 2016 Tesla's score is comparable to that of the others.

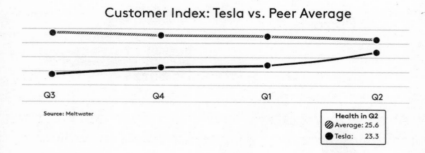

**Customer Index: Tesla vs. Peer Average**

Q3      Q4      Q1      Q2

Source: Meltwater

Health in Q2
Average: 25.6
Tesla: 23.3

Social media are also very suitable for measuring the strength of a brand. Below is the relative footprint of competing fast-food brands on Twitter and Instagram from

May 2015 to May 2016. From the pie chart we can see that McDonald's has four times more social media coverage than its closest rival, Burger King, despite only having twice the number of physical outlets. Similarly, one can see that Pizza Hut has twice the coverage of its competitor Domino's, with only 50 per cent more restaurants.

## Burgers

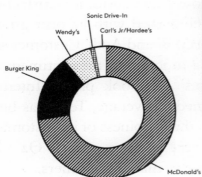

| Rank | | Brand | Share of Voice | #US Stores |
|---|---|---|---|---|
| 1 | | McDonald's | 73.8% | 14,350 |
| 2 | | Burger King | 18.1% | 7,142 |
| 3 | | Wendy's | 6.2% | 5,780 |
| 4 | | Carl's Jr/ Hardees | 1.4% | 2,915 |
| 5 | | Sonic Drive-In | 0.5% | 3,517 |

Source: Meltwater

## Pizza

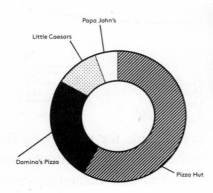

| Rank | | Brand | Share of Voice | #US Stores |
|---|---|---|---|---|
| 1 | | Pizza Hut | 59.2% | 7,863 |
| 2 | | Domino's Pizza | 26.2% | 5,067 |
| 3 | | Little Caesars | 10.3% | 4,025 |
| 4 | | Papa John's | 4.4% | 3,250 |

Source: Meltwater

Social media can also be used to understand the main focus of a brand. Consider the word clouds of the car brands Aston Martin and Rolls-Royce created by news and social media coverage during 2015. The size of the words illustrates how much they have dominated conversations. We can see the different priorities of the two brands straight away. While Aston Martin's word cloud illustrates an emphasis on 'celebrity' and endorsements, Rolls-Royce's is primarily concerned with export markets and industry. To understand this difference it is important to appreciate that Rolls-Royce is much more than just a car brand and that it is focused on promoting a range of products, including aero engines, power systems and nuclear plants.

## *Online ad spend*

Another interesting trail of online breadcrumbs to follow is search engine marketing (SEM), or so-called pay-per-click (PPC) spending. Such spending can be estimated because online search terms are auctioned out in real time, where everyone can see the inventory and going price. eMarketer estimates search spend to have been nearly half (46 per cent) of the total $58.12 billion digital ad-spend market in 2015,[10] so although search spend doesn't tell the full story, it is a very interesting metric to track for most companies.

Tracking your competitors' search spend and how it is trending over time and broken down by countries and product lines can provide invaluable competitive insights. The illustration below estimated SEM spend by Tesla and the same peer group we saw earlier in Q2 2016. Interesting to note is that Tesla is spending almost nothing on online advertisements. BMW, however, is outspending all its competitors on nearly all continents.

## Advertising by Region

| | Tesla | BMW | Audi | Mercedes |
|---|---|---|---|---|
| Asia | $0 | $22K | $41K | $0 |
| Europe | $0 | $431K | $364K | $10K |
| North America | $0 | $3M | $2M | $2M |
| Oceania | $0 | $28K | $23K | $2K |
| South America | $0 | $4K | $0 | $0 |

Source: Meltwater

### *Web traffic and app downloads*

Another commonly used metric for competitive intelligence is web traffic. Web traffic data is not easy to get hold of, but there are third-party companies such as Comscore that estimate website visits. In a similar fashion you can use Google AdWords to see how often your company brands are searched. Compare this data with that of your competitors. If app downloads are important to you, a commonly used service is App Annie. Web traffic, search volume and app downloads are all measures of the level of demand for your products.

Below is last year's ranking history from App Annie for downloads of a handful of popular apps. The ranking is a measure of how popular the apps are, compared with other apps in their category. Such ranking development is an indicator of whether an app is on the up or not.

It is clear that Evernote is on a downward trend, moving from around 500 in popularity down to 1000. WhatsApp is also dropping, although not so drastically, slipping from 10 down to around 25. Dropbox is pretty steady, but looks like it is on a slow downward trend. The only app showing a positive trend is Snapchat. A year ago it was ranked 5. In Q4 2015 it went through a phase where its ranking jumped up and down, but since Q1 2016 it has seen a steady improvement.

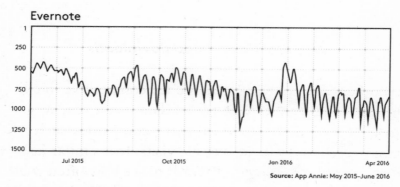

Source: App Annie: May 2015–June 2016

Evernote is seeing a downward trend.

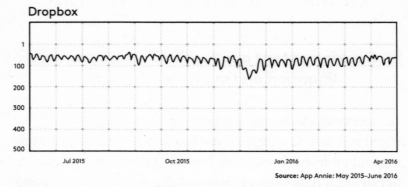

**Source:** App Annie: May 2015–2016

Dropbox is pretty steady, but one can argue there is a slight downward trend since the beginning of 2016.

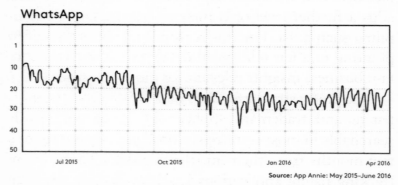

**Source:** App Annie: May 2015–June 2016

WhatsApp saw a drop between the second and third quarter of 2015 and has not been able to recover since.

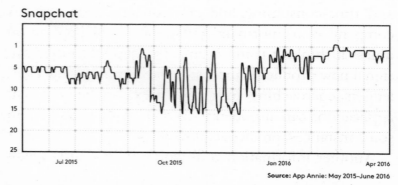

**Source:** App Annie: May 2015–June 2016

Snapchat has been on a positive trend since the beginning of 2016.

## *Tracking patent applications, credit ratings, litigation and import declarations*

In addition to the data types we have discussed so far there is a whole range of data available online containing valuable business insights. To create an exhaustive list of such data types is beyond the scope of this book, as any such list will vary widely from one industry to another. The continual appearance of new data online adds a further level of complexity to the task of compiling such a list. For this reason I will limit myself to pointing to a few additional data types that could contain business insights relevant for most industries.

One pretty straightforward data type in this regard is patent and trademark applications. They are readily searchable in most countries, although there is a lag of a few months from their initial filing date. The value of tracking patent applications is self-evident: it offers an understanding of your competitors' strategic purpose. Patents and trademark applications are both laborious and time-consuming and consequently expensive. A company won't normally pursue a patent application unless it thinks it is important. Patent applications can signal new product launches or the arrival of new challengers encroaching into your area. Studying patent applications can also identify acquisition targets and, in some instances, predict acquisitions.

Another information trail worth following is credit

ratings and company financials. Many companies regularly track the credit ratings or financials of their key and new clients. Credit ratings are equally valuable for keeping tabs on suppliers, partners and other companies in your sphere of business. One of the weaknesses with credit ratings is, of course, that they are not an exact science and that they are lagging indicators.

Litigation is sadly becoming almost a normal practice when running a business – particularly in the US. Information about litigation is often accessible online. The possible gains from studying legal processes are multiple. First, the disputing parties are required to reveal information that might otherwise not be publicly available; second, litigation can send a strong signal that something is to be gained or protected; and third, litigation represents a financial risk for one or both of the parties. And if your business is dependent on a company that is involved in litigation, then it's worth staying on top of the issue.

In the US, shipping companies have to register the contents of the containers they're moving via a document known as a Bill of Lading. Other countries have similar practices. This public record identifies the importer or exporter, including a brief description of the goods or commodities or their commercial value. Import–export data is useful in complex businesses such as the auto industry, which rely on large shipments of raw materials, often across long distances. Such information can be used, for example, to predict future sales volumes of Tesla cars. If you know what the company is importing, it's possible to compare this with historic sales and raw material data and extrapolate what will happen further down the line. For example, a big spike in raw materials will mean that eight months later (the general time-lag between raw materials and the finished car) there will be a certain number of new Tesla cars on the road.

| Online breadcrumbs to follow |
| --- |
| Company websites |
| News |
| Social |
| Job postings |
| Social network connections |
| Online ad spend |
| Web traffic |
| Patent filings and trademarks |
| Credit ratings and company financials |
| Court documents and other public records |

## *The remarkable tale of Apple told by its boilerplate*

So far in this chapter we have discussed the trail of online breadcrumbs that we leave behind, as individuals and as companies. To end this chapter I will show how powerful a simple analysis of such trails can be over time.

For my analysis I will limit myself to an obscure little fingerprint that every company inserts at the bottom of its press releases. It is a short description of the company and is often referred to as a press release 'boilerplate'.

The reason why this boilerplate is interesting is that it gives a very condensed description of what the company does or aspires to do, and is usually limited to a few sentences. These sentences are crafted very deliberately to convey strategic positioning and intent.

Studying the boilerplate in Apple's press releases is a fascinating read, capturing fifteen years of consumer technology history. Apple is highly structured in its approach, consistently using two to three sentences to describe its business. Tracking the development from year to year, we can see how the tech company's strategy and product focus have evolved from computers to personal computing devices. We can also see how Apple's struggles and successes shine through in the choice of tone and language.

In 1997 Apple was in dire straits. Stock was trading at a ten-year low,[11] the Macintosh was outdated, its personal digital assistant (the Newton) had flopped, and the company asked its second CEO in two years to leave. Steve Jobs was brought back to save the company, but Apple was in serious financial trouble and running out of money. A helping hand came from the most unlikely of sources when arch-nemesis Microsoft secured the long-term viability of Apple by investing $150 million and pledging support for the Office Suite for the Macintosh platform for the next five years.[12]

In January 2000 the difficulties and lack of confidence were evident in the Apple boilerplate:

> Apple ignited the personal computer revolution in the 1970s with the Apple II, and reinvented the personal computer in the 1980s with the Macintosh. Apple is now recommitted to its original mission to bring the best personal computing products and support to students, educators, designers, scientists, engineers, businesspersons and consumers in over 140 countries around the world.

The boilerplate starts with a reference to historic accomplishments dating back thirty years and moves on to its recommitment 'to its original mission'. It's as though Apple is telling us, 'Remember how great we were? Now we are working hard to become as great as we used to be.'

Over the next four years Apple experienced a lot of ups and downs. It made progress on renewing its product portfolio, but financials were bumpy. In 2004 Apple ended a seven-year period of stagnation with a solid 33 per cent revenue growth and produced its highest revenue figures since 1996. This increased confidence was evident in the new boilerplate:

> Apple ignited the personal computer revolution in the 1970s with the Apple II, and reinvented the personal

computer in the 1980s with the Macintosh. Today, Apple continues to lead the industry in innovation with its award-winning desktop and notebook computers, OS X operating system, and iLife and professional applications. Apple is also spearheading the digital music revolution with its iPod portable music players and iTunes online store.

Apple was still clinging to its old laurels, but the language had become noticeably bolder in describing the current state of affairs. Also noteworthy is the introduction of a third sentence, highlighting the iPod. Interestingly the reference to the iPod came three years after its actual launch. In future Apple would be a lot more confident about referring to its new product.

On 29 June 2007 the iPhone was launched, receiving universal rave reviews for its ground-breaking design and technology. Apple's revenue grew to three times that of the record-breaking 2004. The good times were back. Sales and profits were soaring, and it showed in the choice of language. In July that year Apple proudly added a proclamation of its iPhone to its boilerplate:

Apple ignited the personal computer revolution in the 1970s with the Apple II, and reinvented the personal computer in the 1980s with the Macintosh. Today, Apple continues to lead the industry in innovation with its award-winning computers, OS X operating system and iLife and professional applications. Apple is also spearheading the digital media revolution with its iPod portable music and video players and iTunes online store, and has entered the mobile phone market this year with its revolutionary iPhone.

On 26 May 2010 Apple's market value overtook that of Microsoft. In Q3 Apple's revenue exceeded for the first time that of its Seattle-based rival. In December 2010 the Apple boilerplate received an overhaul. The language was radically changed. References to historical glories were dropped and replaced by an upbeat description of present-day accomplishments. The hesitation of the past was replaced with language boasting about its 'revolutionary' and 'magical' products:

Apple designs Macs, the best personal computers in the world, along with OS X, iLife, iWork, and professional software. Apple leads the digital music revolution with its iPods and iTunes online store. Apple is reinventing the mobile phone with its revolutionary iPhone and App Store, and has recently introduced its magical iPad which is defining the future of mobile media and computing devices.

In April 2015 Apple became the most valuable company in the world, with a market value of $770 billion.[13] Its share price had risen 24,500 per cent from its lowest point in 1997. The boilerplate was once more rewritten, and in June 2015 it read:

Apple revolutionized personal technology with the introduction of the Macintosh in 1984. Today Apple leads the world in innovation, with iPhone, iPad, Mac, Apple Watch and Apple TV. Apple's four software platforms – iOS, OS X, watchOS and TVOS – provide seamless experiences across all Apple devices and empower people with breakthrough services including the App Store, Apple Music, Apple Pay and iCloud. Apple's 100,000 employees are dedicated to making the best products on earth, and to leaving the world better than we found it.

The language has come full circle: the historic accomplishments are brought back to describe Apple's heritage. The Apple of today is described as a supreme global ruler of a tightly knit consumer ecosystem of devices, software, platforms and services. The forward-looking third sentence is now replaced with a (continued) dedication to making the world better, a statement that Apple fans would find reassuring and that Apple sceptics would describe as hubris.

|  | 1st Sentence | 2nd Sentence | 3rd Sentence |
|---|---|---|---|
| January 2000 | Apple ignited the personal computer revolution in the 1970s with the Apple II, and reinvented the personal computer in the 1980s with the Macintosh. | Apple is now recommitted to its original mission to bring the best personal computing products and support to students, educators, designers, scientists, engineers, businesspersons and consumers in over 140 countries around the world. | |
| December 2000 | Apple ignited the personal computer revolution in the 1970s with the Apple II, and reinvented the personal computer in the 1980s with the Macintosh. | Apple is committed to bringing the best personal computing experience to students, educators, creative professionals and consumers around the world through its innovative hardware, software and internet offerings. | |
| December 2004 | Apple ignited the personal computer revolution in the 1970s with the Apple II, and reinvented the personal computer in the 1980s with the Macintosh. | Today, Apple continues to lead the industry in innovation with its award-winning desktop and notebook computers, OS X operating system, and iLife and professional applications. | Apple is also spearheading the digital music revolution with its iPod portable music players and iTunes online store. |
| July 2007 | Apple ignited the personal computer revolution in the 1970s with the Apple II, and reinvented the personal computer in the 1980s with the Macintosh. | Today, Apple continues to lead the industry in innovation with its award-winning computers, OS X operating system and iLife and professional applications. | Apple is also spearheading the digital media revolution with its iPod portable music and video players and iTunes online store, and has entered the mobile phone market this year with its revolutionary iPhone. |

| | 1st Sentence | 2nd Sentence | 3rd Sentence |
|---|---|---|---|
| December 2010 | Apple designs Macs, the best personal computers in the world, along with OS X, iLife, iWork, and professional software. | Apple leads the digital music revolution with its iPods and iTunes online store. | Apple is reinventing the mobile phone with its revolutionary iPhone and App Store, and has recently introduced its magical iPad which is defining the future of mobile media and computing devices. |
| June 2015 | Apple revolutionized personal technology with the introduction of the Macintosh in 1984. | Today Apple leads the world in innovation, with iPhone, iPad, Mac, Apple Watch and Apple TV. Apple's four software platforms – iOS, OS X, watchOS and TVOS – provide seamless experiences across all Apple devices and empower people with breakthrough services including the App Store, Apple Music, Apple Pay and iCloud. | Apple's 100,000 employees are dedicated to making the best products on earth, and to leaving the world better than we found it. |

The analysis of Apple's boilerplate shows how much information can be found in the online trails companies leave behind. The world has changed. Today we have access to information online that we did not have just a few years ago. The internet has become a treasure trove of business insights ready to be mined.

In the rest of the book we will study how analysis of online breadcrumbs will transform corporate decision-making and the way that companies are run and governed.

# Chapter Two

# Mining Internal Data Is Looking at the Past

In 1977 a college dropout named Larry Ellison founded a start-up which he called Software Development Laboratories. In his previous job at Ampex, an electronics company, he had read a paper by the British computer scientist Edgar Frank Codd, who, while working for IBM in 1970, had written 'A Relational Model for Large Shared Data Banks'. Ellison worked on a number of projects for Ampex, including a database for the CIA, which he called Oracle, the name which he eventually gave his company.

The business, based in Redwood Shores, California, would come to dominate the database and enterprise software market commonly referred to as Enterprise Resource Planning (ERP). Today Oracle is one of the world's most powerful tech companies. For its 2015 fiscal year Oracle posted revenue of $38.2 billion and profits of $10 billion.[1]

Oracle's founder, Larry Ellison, is not as famous as Apple's Steve Jobs or Microsoft's Bill Gates, but he has shaped the world we live in as much as either of them. Before Oracle, company data was buried in silos and hard to access. Some data was stored in mainframes or typed and handwritten on paper in binders. Most of the data was not in a usable format, making it impossible to analyse for meaning and insight. The advent of ERP systems meant that this internal data was slowly digitized. Indeed, by 2005, 80 per cent of Fortune 500 companies had installed, or were in the process of implementing, a company-wide ERP system.[2]

As the market started to demand software customized for different functional needs – such as customer relationship management (CRM), finance, human resources (HR), supply chain and business intelligence (BI) – Ellison embarked on an unprecedented decade-long acquisition spree to the tune of $35 billion. The acquisitions added expertise in workflow, business, logic, visualization and reporting on top of Oracle's database and made it the most trusted enterprise software company in the world. In Chapter 13 we will see how history repeats itself and will study these acquisitions in more detail.

Today we're so used to enterprise software that it's easy to forget that it has only been around since the mid-1990s. Today executives are completely reliant on their ERP system for understanding their business performance. What is our client retention in Europe like? What are the latest productivity numbers per salesperson? What is the profit contribution of our newest business division? Where is our growth coming from today? How do we get the largest return on investment? The answers to all of these questions can be found in the ERP systems.

Larry Ellison's Oracle has spearheaded an entire new industry of staggering proportions. Global annual corporate IT spend, including servers, devices, enterprise software and professional services, reached $3.52 trillion in 2015, according to the technology research company Gartner.[3] To put this number in perspective, that is bigger than the global car industry!

If Steve Jobs revolutionized computing for consumers, then Larry Ellison did the same thing for enterprise. As of January 2016 Oracle employs 133,000 people and is run by 98 per cent of the Fortune 500 companies.[4] For more than forty years Ellison has been one of Silicon Valley's most influential individuals. Beyond Oracle, he has played an instrumental role in a number of Silicon Valley's success stories, including Salesforce and Net-Suite, both leading cloud-based enterprise software companies.

In January 2016 Ellison was ranked the fifth-wealthiest person in the world by *Forbes Magazine*, with a net worth of $54 billion, dwarfing the founders of Facebook, Google and Amazon, and eclipsed only by Bill Gates among IT entrepreneurs.

Larry Ellison built his wealth on changing the way companies make decisions. His software transformed the internal world of companies from a collection of inefficient systems that didn't communicate to a streamlined ERP system where information from all parts of the company could be combined into rigorous analysis and enable thoughtful, data-driven decisions.

## *Internal data is lagging data*

The introduction of ERP systems like Oracle clearly represented a very valuable upgrade from the old paradigm, where executives couldn't access the internal data in an efficient way.

The obvious limitation with ERP systems is that they contain lagging data based on historical events. The figures in financial reports are the end-result of activities and investments that took place in the past. It takes months and sometimes quarters to ramp up a new salesperson. In many industries it takes years of investment to develop and bring a product to market. In our ERP system we can probe and analyse our data down to fine-tuned granularity, but, for all our efforts, the only insights we will find will be historical.

A key thesis of this book is that we need to be careful with how we use our ERP software. Over-reliance on these systems can be dangerous and create a world-view limited by the information that can be found in our internal systems. It is easy to be swayed by captivating graphs and analysis, but we have to bear in mind that our ERP system can only answer a few of the questions we have to ask ourselves when making important decisions.

The current situation is not present in the figures we find in our ERP system. Neither is recent investment by our competitors and recent industry development. For all its persuasive rigour, internal data has clear limitations when making decisions about the future. The following example illustrates this well.

In 2012, for the third year running, Meltwater's Canadian office performed badly, in stark contrast to the performance of the rest of the company. We lost money, we didn't grow and retention of people was the worst in the company.

In January 2013 we had a heated discussion at a Meltwater board meeting. Because of these poor figures, our external board members were pushing hard to close down in Canada and invest our dollars in other markets instead. After all, it was our smallest business unit and insignificant. I argued that there was nothing wrong with the Canadian market. The competitive landscape was attractive, and its maturity was well above other markets we thrived in. I argued that this was an internal issue because we did not have the right management in place. I presented an alternative strategy with new management and a doubling down on our investments.

Eventually the board supported my plan, and within three years Canada leapt from the twentieth and worst-performing business unit within Meltwater to the fifth-best, entering 2016 with an impressive 55 per cent annual growth rate.

At the Meltwater board we talk about this incident from time to time. We use it to remind ourselves that there is only so much that can be accomplished by poring over historical data – partly because history doesn't necessarily predict the future, and partly because there is only so much that can be captured in a spreadsheet. Running a company is a complex endeavour. The biggest factor is always your people. Their confidence, enthusiasm and conviction are always the most important factors in your future business performance.

### *The insular bias*

Another problem with ERP systems is that you study your company's internal data in isolation. You don't get current information about what your competition is doing. You don't get reliable information about industry trends. You create a world-view based on what you see through the lens of your historical operational efficiency.

Internal analyses in isolation can create a misguided understanding of your competitive situation. Say the price you are able to get for your product in the French market drops over a twelve-month period. Is this due to weaker demand in the market, increased competition or lower confidence in your French sales organization? From just looking at your internal data it would be very difficult to know. And that is a big problem because without properly understanding the root cause of the issue it is hard to take appropriate action.

More often than not, management don't have – or don't make the effort to get – third-party data to help them interpret their internal data. Instead they are influenced by preconceived ideas or beliefs that may or may not be entirely accurate.

This insular bias is fortified as analysis travels up through the organization. When a report reaches the company board, the underlying facts have been analysed, structured and packaged through many layers of management. At each level, data is curated to support the narrative each level of management wants to communicate. Some data will be amplified; other data will be muted. As a report travels upwards through a company, there is a tendency for the facts to become weaker and the narrative stronger.

Being too internally focused is dangerous, given the pace with which the world is changing today. Forty per cent of the Fortune 500 companies in the year 2000 were gone ten years later.[5] This destructive development seems to accelerate. In 2014 Dennis Hanno, Dean of Babson School of Business in Wellesley, Massachusetts, predicted that half of the Fortune 500 companies at that time would also be gone within a decade.

There are many tales about great companies that have crumbled because they were not able to adapt quickly enough. This is not because there was a lack of data showing their steady decline. Their problem lay with fighting preconceived beliefs and breaking through their internal bias.

## *The rise and fall of BlackBerry*

When BlackBerry's joint CEOs, Mike Lazaridis and Jim Balsillie, first saw the iPhone in January 2007, they were convinced that the device didn't pose a threat to their mobile services company, according to *Losing the Signal: The Untold Story behind the Extraordinary Rise and Spectacular Fall of BlackBerry*, by Jacquie McNish and Sean Silcoff.[6] They considered their own mobile devices to be a far better proposition for business users: the iPhone was more expensive, had a much shorter battery life, a 2G radio and a touchscreen keyboard. How many business users would go for that? They'd be on a sales call in Cleveland and by the time they were out of the rental car park they'd need to recharge.

And in the short term BlackBerry's executives were right. The Canadian phone producer grew steadily by delighting the professional business users with its user-friendly keyboard, integrated corporate security and innovative messaging system, called BBM. By Q1 2009 BlackBerry had become standard for the lucrative business segment, with a market share of 55 per cent in the US and 20 per cent globally.[7]

During the next three years, despite tremendous growth, the market was running away from the Canadian handset manufacturer. People had moved on to a new generation of smartphones with a touch screen instead of a keyboard.

In Q1 2012 growth took a brutal hit. Delays in new product releases were cited as one of the reasons for this, but it was clear from the stagnating user growth that the consumer had developed a strong appetite for competing products. Q1 2012 revenue was $2.8 billion, down 33 per cent from the previous quarter and down 43 per cent from the year before. So worrying was the outlook that the new CEO of RIM (the company that produces the BlackBerry), Thorstein Heins, laid off 4,500 people, nearly 40 per cent of the workforce. 'There is nothing wrong with the company as it exists right now,' he insisted in an interview with the Canadian Broadcasting Radio Corp.[8] 'Rather, we believe RIM is a company at the beginning of a transition that we expect will once again change the way people communicate. [ . . . ] As we prepare to launch our new mobile platform, BlackBerry 10, in the first quarter of next year, we expect to empower people as never before.'

Thorstein Heins's predictions didn't come true. BlackBerry's development took instead a nose-dive. In September 2013 BlackBerry announced a second-quarter net loss of close to a billion dollars owing to poor sales of one particular model, the Z10.[9] BlackBerry was at this point haemorrhaging users and market share. By the end of the year the market share had plummeted to 0.6 per cent globally. The once admired innovation leader in the smartphone sector had been wiped out.

The implosion of the Canadian telco and handset manufacturer is one of the most dramatic corporate demises of recent times. The speed at which the company moved from dominating the corporate mobile phone market to fighting for its very existence took both insiders and market watchers by surprise.

The tale of BlackBerry is an excellent example of the limitations of internal company data. From the time the first iPhone was unveiled in 2007 to the fatal quarterly report for Q1 2012, BlackBerry's users grew almost tenfold (!), from 8 million to 77 million. Equally impressive is the quarterly revenue growth. BlackBerry hit $1 billion in quarterly revenue in Q1 2007 and shot up to $5.5 billion by Q1 2011, growing by between 40 and 100 per cent year-on-year in most quarters.

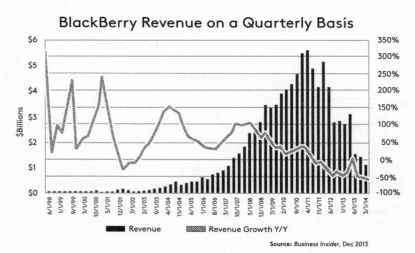

Source: *Business Insider*, Dec 2013

BlackBerry's revenue development. Revenue grew strongly all the way to its peak in Q1 2011, with $5.5 billion in quarterly revenue. In spite of the strong growth, the company was losing market share and would soon be in trouble.

Looking at BlackBerry's internal figures alone, one would think that BlackBerry was going from one victory to another. It turns out the internal data didn't tell the whole story. By definition, internal data is biased; it contains rich data about your company, but no direct information about the market and your competitors.

Studying the market share development, the picture looks quite different. Now it is obvious that the problems had started to appear as far back as Q1 2009. Up until that point BlackBerry had been seeing strong growth and a steady increase in market share, peaking at 20 per cent globally, but from this point the development was very concerning. US market share dropped from 55 per cent in Q1 2009 to 12 per cent in less than two years. Globally, the drop in market share was less rapid, but within three years it had plunged to obscurity internationally too.

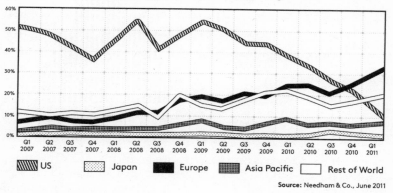

**BlackBerry Market Share by Region**

Source: Needham & Co., June 2011

Blackberry's US market share took a nose dive from Q1 2009. This negative development was an early warning of BlackBerry's fall.

## BlackBerry Share of Shipments

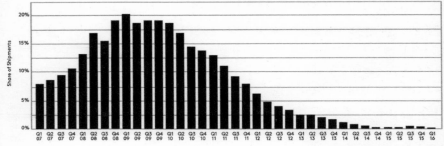

Source: Statista via Fortune, June 2011

BlackBerry's global market share rose steadily through Q1 2009, two years after the launch of Apple's iPhone. From Q1 2010, however, BlackBerry's market share quickly eroded.

A further study of the different handset makers' individual faith paints an even more nuanced picture. Nokia (Symbian) and BlackBerry (RIM) were the big losers, whereas Apple and the Android phones are the winners. Android won the volume game, with a growth from about 10 per cent in 2010 to an incredible 80 per cent in 2013. When it comes to profitability, though, industry analysts agree that Apple is dominant, in spite of being consistently at a relatively modest market share of 15 to 20 per cent.

According to analyst firm Strategy Analytics, Apple's iPhone secured $11.4 billion profit for Q4 2013, which is more than 70 per cent of the profitability of the entire industry. One year later, in Q4 2014, Apple had increased their iPhone profit to $18.8 billion and a staggering 89 per cent of the total profit pool.

# Smartphone Market Share in %
## Quarterly, by operating system

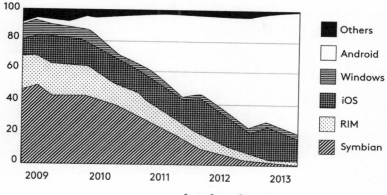

Source: Reuters, Gartner, Sept 2013

As the smartphone market went through dramatic changes between 2009 and 2013, Symbian and RIM were the big losers. The winners were Apple and Android.

| Global Smartphone Operating Profit (US$, Billions) | Q4 2013 | Q4 2014 |
|---|---|---|
| Apple iOS | 11.4 | 18.8 |
| Android | 4.8 | 2.4 |
| Microsoft | 0.0 | 0.0 |
| BlackBerry | 0.0 | 0.0 |
| Others | 0.0 | 0.0 |
| Total | 16.2 | 21.2 |

| Global Smartphone Operating Profit Share | Q4 2013 | Q4 2014 |
|---|---|---|
| Apple iOS | 70.5% | 88.7% |
| Android | 29.5% | 11.3% |
| Microsoft | 0.0% | 0.0% |
| BlackBerry | 0.0% | 0.0% |
| Others | 0.0% | 0.0% |
| Total | 100.0% | 100.0% |
| Total Growth Year-over-Year | – | 31.4% |

Although Android developed a dominant market share of almost 80 per cent by Q4 2013, Apple was able to capture most of the profit. In Q4 Apple secured 89 per cent of the total industry profit despite having a market share of less than 20 per cent.

The demise of BlackBerry is complex, but at its heart the company remained too focused on what it used to excel at – physical keyboards and security – and was not able to adapt quickly enough when the market changed. In spite of impressive growth, the company was losing market share because the competitors were growing faster. In the end BlackBerry would be reduced to irrelevance.

Competitors fuelled their growth by catering to the new generation of smartphone users better. BlackBerry didn't embrace the new user demands, such as browsing the internet and apps for consuming media and services. The BlackBerry browser was a miserable online experience, and their app effort, when it arrived, was too little and too late. BlackBerry were stuck in their focus on creating a phone for productivity while the competition, spearheaded by Apple, appealed to the user's emotional side with slick design, a lush high-resolution colour screen and an innovative touch interface unlike anything anyone had seen before.

RIM's chief technology officer, David Yach, admitted that the company didn't anticipate iPhone's popularity. He told *The Wall Street Journal*: 'By all rights the product should have failed, but it did not. I learned that beauty matters [. . .] RIM was caught incredulous that people wanted to buy this thing.'[10]

BlackBerry relied too much on historical success recipes and grossly underestimated its competition. Its staggering revenue growth through 2011 gave the company a false sense of confidence, and it failed to acknowledge that its market share had plummeted from its peak in Q1 2009. From its 2011 record revenue Black-Berry dropped more than 80 per cent in revenue within three years and would never recover. It failed to adjust to changing market demands. BlackBerry's historical success with the keyboard interface created an internal bias that drove the company off a cliff.

At the Battle of Copenhagen in 1801 Lord Nelson, then a vice-admiral in the British fleet, leading the main attack against the Danes, is famously said to have put his telescope to his blind eye to avoid seeing flags signalling him to withdraw. Nelson's mind was set, and he refused to be distracted from his course.

For all its promise of converting corporate decision-making from the realm of gut feeling to a rigorous discipline based on facts, enterprise software has inherent weaknesses. The internal data captured represents only a narrow slice of information influencing your company's future. The insights extracted from these numbers will always suffer from internal biases and follow a subjective narrative distilled by layers of managers and executives.

In the rest of the book we will discuss the biggest blind spot in contemporary decision-making and how a new decision paradigm is necessary in order to embrace a new digital reality. This will in turn give rise to an entirely new software category that will transform executive decision-making just as much as the introduction of enterprise software did in its time.

# Chapter Three

# Mining External Data Is Looking into the Future

RaceTrac is one of the US's largest privately owned companies, with sales in 2016 of $7.5 billion and convenience stores and petrol stations across twelve states.[1] The company, based in Atlanta, Georgia, was founded in 1934 and has been run by three generations of the Bolch family: Carl Bolch, Carl Bolch Jr and Allison Moran, who took over as CEO in 2012.

RaceTrac's business was in great shape, but Moran knew that there was an opportunity to understand consumer demand more holistically through the use of external data, so that she could get a sense of what factors would affect what would sell – and what wouldn't. Margins in the convenience store industry are tight, so having low-demand products on the shelves can have a significant impact; shelf space is at a premium as most of RaceTrac's stores occupy less than 5,000 square feet.

Traditionally forecasting and planning for RaceTrac's more than 650 company-owned and third-party contract-operated stores had been done by the CEO, CFO and various operational teams. When Moran took over, she decided that she wanted to expand some of the core capabilities of the company; and one of these was forecasting and predictive modelling.

'We had vast amounts of historical financial information, performance, people metrics, human resources metrics, things of that nature, but really the lion's share of what we looked at was internal data,' says Brad Galland, the director of financial planning and analysis at RaceTrac. 'We decided we wanted to try to get a better understanding of our piece of the world as it related to market share. One year in particular we had double-digit growth. We were looking at our profitability inside of our stores and we started asking the question, "Well, are we just growing with the market or are we beating it?" If we do nothing would we still have double-digit growth?'

In late 2012 RaceTrac turned to the predictive analytics company Prevedere. Together they analysed a wide range of external data signals and discovered that weather data, construction statistics, commodity pricing and manufacturing trends all influenced RaceTrac's future sales.

'It's really impacted our business, especially on the planning side,' Galland says. 'Beforehand, when we sat down to do an annual financial forecast it was based on, "Okay sales last year were X – if we say X plus an additional 5 per cent that's more or less where we think we're going to be. That's based on our various category teams putting their projections together and saying, yeah, you know, we think we're going to grow beverages by 10 per cent. We think we're going to grow this candy category by 12 per cent." That is all well and good, except for there were a lot of, "I thinks" and "we should be able to do that" and "that seems like a reasonable target".

'Now, we have something that is grounded in factual reality. We can now say, with some degree of certainty, we feel pretty confident that our year-to-year sales are going to increase by 9.7 per cent. Based on sales we can anticipate profit margins, down to a level of net profitability. That's pretty significant.'

Mining external data points enabled RaceTrac to determine leading performance indicators in each of the product categories and regions it operates in, tuning out the noise and zeroing in on the indices that offered a true forecast. RaceTrac had detailed information on guest count and, by combining that with the products that strongly correlated with the external indicators, it was able to build a powerful regression model that reduced the forecasting error by 15 per cent.

RaceTrac is a great example of a business that has understood the value of looking at external data. In external data they found forward-looking information that complemented their ERP analysis. Through regression modelling they were able to identify key external factors that drove their sales. By including these in their forecasting processes they could replace internal guesswork and significantly increase precision in their revenue forecasts.

## *External online data is the biggest blind spot in corporate decision-making today*

The rigour with which RaceTrac takes advantage of external data is unusual at present. The uncomfortable truth is that most companies today are still surprisingly ad hoc when it comes to taking advantage of the wealth of business insights available online.

Over the last couple of decades the World Wide Web has become one of the most valuable sources for forward-looking information. Grossly underutilized, it has also become the biggest blind spot in corporate decision-making.

Enterprise software has replaced the guesswork of the past and given birth to an entirely new industry helping companies measure their productivity and make data-driven decisions based on their internal data. The next frontier is to mine external data with the same rigour.

Big data and predictive analytics have become common C-suite jargon. In spite of all the hype, many companies struggle to work out how to apply these new technologies practically in a way that creates real value. The obvious next step for companies to become more rigorous is for them to look externally. Every company has external factors that impact future business performance positively and negatively. Mining external data to understand these is like having a stethoscope listening into Porter's Five Forces in real time.

Companies that embrace this opportunity will have a huge advantage. Companies that don't are running blind.

## An example of a company that ignored external data: the rise and fall of the company that invented the digital camera

In December 1975 Steven Sasson, a twenty-five-year-old electrical engineer, invented a game-changing product that would eventually bring his employer, which had 120,000 employees and almost a hundred years of global dominance in its field, to its knees. 'Innovation best comes from people who really know nothing about the topic,' said Sasson. Just a year or so after his graduation from Rensselaer Polytechnic Institute, he was asked by his manager to experiment with some new chipsets recently made available by Fairchild Semiconductors. The experiment would later be referred to as US Patent 4,131,919 – more commonly known as the digital camera.

Sasson's managers were impressed by his invention but decided not to pursue the technology as it could impact the company's primary source of revenue, which was photographic film. Sasson's employer was the revered Eastman Kodak. The company was founded in 1888 by George Eastman, based on his innovations in film rolls for still photos. By offering affordable cameras as 'convenient to use as the pencil', Kodak freed photography from the professional portrait studio, releasing the technology into the everyday lives of ordinary Americans and later all over the world. Eastman was an astute businessman. When competition heated up in the camera industry, he focused on making high-quality, affordable film and thereby transforming potential competitors into de facto business partners. In the process he created a global empire that would last for over a century. At its peak in 1996 Kodak had more than two-thirds global market share, a record revenue of $16 billion and a market value of $31 billion. At the time Kodak was the fifth most valuable brand in the world.[2]

Only fifteen years later it was all over. On 29 January 2012 Kodak filed for bankruptcy. The once legendary company crumbled because it hadn't grasped how the outside world was changing. Kodak, the inventor of the digital camera, had all the technology and know-how to adjust to a digital world. However, its executives hung on to their old beliefs. They ignored all the external data and refused to give up their belief in the superiority of analog films and hard prints. This turned out to be fatal.

The vision of Antonio Pérez, who was appointed chairman and CEO in 2005 to revive the struggling giant, illustrates how out of touch Kodak's top executives were with the challenges to their existing business model. His vision was 'to make Kodak do for photos what Apple does for music: help people to organize and manage their personal library of images. In an ideal world, consumers of the future will snap pictures on Kodak's cameras, save them on its memory cards, put them on paper through its printers and edit them on in-store digital kiosks.'[3]

Pérez, a trained electrical engineer and no stranger to technology, failed to recognize how technology was transforming consumer behaviour and old business models. People loved their digital cameras. With a digital camera you could see the photo you had just taken straight away instead of having to wait for the film to be developed and printed. Everyone old enough to have used a camera with analog film remembers the liberating feeling of taking photos for the first time with a digital camera. And as the internet became prolific, the digital photo took on a life that the old photographic negative had never had. Photos could be stored, shared and edited online, making people perfectly happy not to print them on paper any more.

A lot has been written and said about the rise and fall of Kodak, and in hindsight it is easy to have 20/20 vision. However, by studying online data widely available during the tenure of Mr Pérez we will see how many of the most important macro trends were in stark contrast to his vision for the revival of the century-old giant.

# US Analog vs. Digital Camera Sales

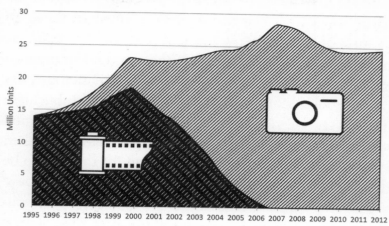

Million Units

30
25
20
15
10
5
0

1995 1996 1997 1998 1999 2000 2001 2002 2003 2004 2005 2006 2007 2008 2009 2010 2011 2012

▨ Analog  ▨ Digital

**Source:** Third Way, April 2014

# Decline of Film

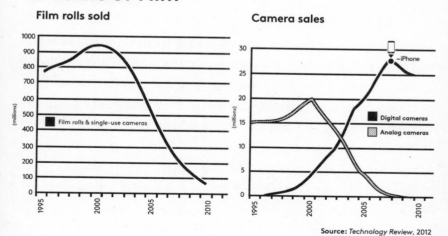

## Film rolls sold

(millions)

1000
900
800
700
600
500
400
300
200
100
0

■ Film rolls & single-use cameras

1995   2000   2005   2010

## Camera sales

(millions)

30
25
20
15
10
5
0

← iPhone

■ Digital cameras
▨ Analog cameras

1995   2000   2005   2010

**Source:** *Technology Review*, 2012

In 2005, when Pérez was appointed CEO, seven years before Kodak filed for bankruptcy, the market share for analog cameras in the US had dropped to 20 per cent. Only five years earlier, analog cameras had been completely dominant, with a market share of 80 per cent. In the same five-year period the number of film rolls sold (Kodak's main revenue source) had dropped by 50 per cent.

In spite of the clear market trends, Kodak was unwilling to adapt. It insisted on sticking with its old business models instead of looking at what the consumers wanted. Dr Kamal Munir, Reader in Strategy and Policy at Cambridge University, wrote in *The Wall Street Journal Europe* after Kodak's bankruptcy filing: 'Unwilling to let go of the extremely lucrative film business with gross margins of nearly 70%, it tried for many years to prolong the life of film through smaller cameras and digitally coded film and hybrid technologies such as Photo CD.'[4]

The tale of Kodak shows how external data was reliably reporting on a changing world that had moved from analog to digital photography. At its heart Kodak was a chemical company producing photographic films and refused to accept the story told by the external data. Kodak's digital image division, locked up in its Rochester headquarters, were tasked with creating synergies with their analog film business instead of doubling down on standalone digital business models.

In spite of Kodak's dominant position in the

photography market – remember the phrase 'a Kodak moment' – Kodak was never able to take part in the huge value creation in the digital photographic market. The irony is that Kodak owned one of the largest online photo services, Kodak Gallery. At its peak in 2008 it had more than 60 million members and 'billions' of photos under management, according to Director of Communication Liz Scanlon. After Kodak's bankruptcy filing in 2012, Kodak Gallery was sold to Shutterfly, its main rival, for $23.8 million.[5]

## An example of a company that paid careful attention to external data: the creation of the world's winner in digital photography

In March 2010 a start-up called Burbn secured $500,000 in funding from Baseline Ventures and Andreessen Horowitz.[6] Burbn was a location-based check-in app modelled on Foursquare. Users could check in at particular locations, make future plans, earn points for hanging out with friends and post pictures of their meetings. But the app never took off.

The founders, Kevin Systrom and Mike Krieger, didn't give up and continued to tweak the app. They discovered that people weren't using Burbn's check-in features at all. What they were using were the app's photo-sharing features. Kevin and Mike realized that they had stumbled on something interesting. They honed in on the photo-sharing and by studying the players in the photo-sharing space they concluded there was a space between the cool Hipstamatic, with its user-friendly filters, and Facebook, whose photo app still had a limited sharing capability.

On 12 October 2010 they launched a simple photo-sharing app that could post a picture in three clicks. The images were confined to a square shape, similar to Kodak Instamatic and Polaroid, and through a set of powerful, one-click filters the original could be enhanced and beautified. The app was named Instagram, and within two months it had more than 1 million users.

On 2 February 2011 Instagram secured $7 million in Series A funding (so named by Silicon Valley investors for the first significant external funding round) from a variety of investors, including Benchmark Capital, Twitter co-founder Jack Dorsey, Google's former head of special initiatives, Chris Sacca, and former CTO of Facebook, Adam D'Angelo.[7] The deal valued Instagram at around $25 million.

Instagram grew quickly, and by 26 September 2011 it had 10 million users;[8] it had also been named iPhone app of the year for 2011 by Apple.[9] On 3 April 2012, when it launched on Google Play, its Android version was downloaded more than a million times in less than a day. That same week Instagram raised $50 million from venture capitalists Sequoia Capital, Thrive Capital and Greylock Partners, valuing the company at $500 million.[10]

Somebody who did pay attention to the success of Instagram was the twenty-six-year-old founder of Facebook, Mark Zuckerberg. Facebook was the world's largest social network, with 850 million users, and had filed two months earlier for IPO planning to raise $5 billion with a valuation of $100 billion, making it one of the largest IPOs in tech history. In spite of this success, Facebook had fallen behind on the mobile platform, letting Instagram capture much of the buzz around photo-sharing. Instagram was a very small company with a dozen or so employees and no revenue, but Zuckerberg felt threatened. The previous summer he had already floated the idea of an acquisition with Kevin Systrom, but Systrom had declined because he wanted to build an independent company.

On Monday, 9 April 2012, three months after Eastman Kodak filed for bankruptcy, Facebook acquired Instagram for $1 billion in cash and shares.[11] While there is no publicly available information on the research that Zuckerberg conducted to inform this decision, it's relevant that the deal happened six days after Instagram's spectacular launch on Google Play. During those six days 5 million users had downloaded Instagram's Android version. At the time of the $1 billion acquisition Instagram had only 27 million users,[12] less than half of what Kodak Gallery had had four years earlier.

Unlike Kodak Gallery, Instagram had formidable growth and was a very hot property. The day after Instagram raised $50 million in capital, Zuckerberg entered a three-day CEO-to-CEO process with Systrom at his home in Palo Alto, California. Zuckerberg secured the acquisition of the photo-sharing sensation by offering a price that Systrom could not say no to.

After the acquisition was announced, Zuckerberg received a lot of criticism. Instagram was eighteen months old, had thirteen employees and no revenue. Admittedly it had almost 30 million users, but they were all using the app for free, and there were no plans for how they would be monetized. The acquisition had apparently also sparked unrest among Facebook shareholders and board members, who thought Zuckerberg was 'immature' and acted 'too much on his own'.[13]

A little over three years later, in September 2015, Instagram reached 400 million users. In his 2015 year-end analysis, RBC Capital Markets analyst Mark Mahaney predicted that Instagram would become 'the story of 2016' for Facebook and estimated the revenue from photo-sharing would reach $2 billion for the year.[14] Bank of America Merrill Lynch analysts Justin Post and Joyce Tran were also bullish on behalf of Instagram. In an analyst brief to its clients in late 2015 they estimated Instagram's value on a standalone basis to be between $30 and $37 billion.[15] Their research showed that Instagram had become the largest social network outside China (aside from Facebook). In their report they wrote: 'If Instagram can follow through and continue growing, it'll make Zuckerberg's $1 billion 2012 purchase look like the greatest steal of all time.'

The story of Instagram is a popular tale of two twenty-something entrepreneurs who turned an initial failure around to create a $1 billion exit in eighteen months without making a single dollar in revenue.

It is also the tale of a global giant who paid close attention to how the world was changing. Instagram was an insignificant company compared with Facebook, but its traction in user growth was available online through services such as App Annie. And Facebook's founder and CEO, Mark Zuckerberg, took notice. In the midst of a hectic period of listing his company to the tune of $100 billion, he identified Instagram as a potential threat that he had to address immediately. Photos were one of the most engaging data types online, and if Instagram was able to continue its user growth, it could one day become a threat even for Facebook. His $1 billion insurance premium turned out to be a 'steal'. It made Facebook the global winner in digital photos and solidified Facebook's position as the undisputed king of social media.

Had Facebook only considered their internal financials, no clues would have been found about a new competitor on the rise in the photo segment. Only through careful studies of external data could Zuckerberg identify the emerging threat from Instagram.

In 1609 Galileo Galilei earned fame and riches by presenting to the Venice establishment a telescope that could be used to see seafaring ships two hours before they could be seen by the naked eye. The military benefits of such a technology were obvious and were deployed with significant success. The benefits for a company that mines external data for forward-looking insights are equally attractive. In Part II of this book a decision paradigm is presented to do this in a systematic way.

# Part Two

## A New Decision Paradigm

## Chapter Four

# Outside Insight:
# A New Decision Paradigm for
# a New Digital Reality

The Volvo Ocean Race (VOR) is one of the toughest sporting events in the world. Over a nine-month period seven teams race from Alicante in Spain around the globe to Gothenburg in Sweden, via ports on every continent.

It first took place in 1973 under the name Whitbread Round the World Race, and now happens every three years. Until recently, characteristics of the individual yacht's design – such as the length of the boat, its weight and its sails – had a significant impact on speed. But the rules of the 2014–15 race were changed to make sure the competition was measuring skill rather than boats. No team had an advantage or a disadvantage because each of the boats was a so-called 'one-design'. The vessels were then constructed by one of four world-class boat-builders. This meant that there was only one variable that determined success: the athletes' prowess as sailors over the 44,580 miles of racing across the Atlantic, Pacific, Indian and Southern oceans.

'We have the longest sporting event on the planet – it's nine months – which means that we have to make decisions based on data constantly,' said Iñigo Aznar, head of commercial partnerships, who has business intelligence as part of his remit. 'The event is unpredictable – we know when we start and when we finish, but we don't know what's going to happen in the middle.'

When the race is in progress, the control centre receives data from the boats every three seconds via satellite technology, and the team uses analytics such as biometrics to monitor the physiological condition of the sailors, each of whom burns 6,000 calories per day – three to four times what an average person uses on an average day.[1] Meteorology data – detecting wind and hazards such as ice – is overseen from a highly sophisticated operations hub based in Alicante, a darkened room full of computer hardware and walls of screens that is part mission control, part media centre.

The VOR produces a significant amount of content – 4,874 minutes of video were exchanged live from the boats in 2014–15 and 265,267MB of emails or satellite airtime was used during the race.[2] All VOR content – which is distributed via traditional media as well as social channels such as YouTube, Twitter and Facebook and the website – is produced, edited and distributed in Alicante. 'We're able to send or receive a video from a boat and send an edited version to media around the world in half an hour,' Aznar said.

In the past, cameras were placed on the boats once the teams had designed and built the vessel. The new generations of boats are more like moving television studios, equipped with five fixed-camera positions and two uplink points wirelessly transmitting the videos in real time. The cameras can be remotely controlled and directed, and the microphones are positioned to enhance recordings whatever the conditions: it's crucial that both the sound equipment and the cameras are protected from the wind and water. There is also a multimedia journalist on every boat recording and interviewing day and night.

'Nowadays you cannot tell a story about something that happened yesterday,' Aznar says. 'Because of social channels everything has to be instant, so we have created a high-quality system to be able to cover the race quickly. That would be like having a journalist inside Lewis Hamilton's Formula One car, asking, "How do you feel?"'

On some legs of the race the crews race day and night for periods of close to three weeks, experiencing moments of extreme physical and mental exhaustion, often in treacherous conditions. On 29 November 2014 the Vestas Wind team ran aground and was stranded on the Cargados Carajos Shoals, about 240 nautical miles north-east of Mauritius in the Indian Ocean. The nine crew members were eventually evacuated; some suffered minor injuries. On-board cameras captured the event in grim but compelling detail.

The VOR has ambitious visions. Aznar says their objective is 'to be the best-performing digital global sports competition in the world'. They have to create value for their sponsors, and to do this they strive for compelling and emotional communication with their global following of millions of people.

'We have to know whether the content is right or not in real time,' Aznar says. 'So, if we launch a video on Facebook, send out a press release or produce an interview, we need to know how it's performing across the globe. Then we can make decisions – we know what kinds of stories are working better. We measure performance, like most sporting events, but our real-time need is stronger.'

Monitoring content performance – knowing what kind of tweets perform best or which photographs have the most engagement on Instagram – involves multiple metrics. The team learned, for instance, that there was a 20 per cent increase in engagement on Facebook when content was posted between 12 p.m. and 2 p.m. And posting between Monday and Friday was better than posting at the weekend. Why? Because the majority of those following the VOR are in the ABC1 demographic and are therefore likely to be in managerial positions; the data suggests that they follow the race from their desks during their lunch hours.

This leads to strategic decisions regarding timing. For instance, when the boats come into port, the VOR team notices a significant drop-off in traffic.

'We postponed some of the most interesting things we had to say for a certain time to maintain the level of reach in different markets,' Aznar says. 'These kinds of data insights help us to make real decisions on how we would drive communications to perform better; and at the end of the day to give more value to our sponsors.'

Most companies have a lot to learn from the Volvo Ocean Race. The nine-month regatta is an operation designed with impressive rigour. In harsh conditions in open sea it uses state-of-the-art technology to collect internal and external information and pushes technology and real-time decision-making to the limit in order to create the best sporting event and the best spectator experience possible.

### The Outside Insight paradigm

Corporate decision-making is due for a major overhaul. At the moment it is dominated by internal data and historical events. It is ignoring the wealth of information available online, and is restricted by a quarterly schedule that is inadequate in today's fast-paced world.

Companies large and small are now learning to make decisions in a similar way to the Volvo Ocean Race. They are investing in understanding the world around them and thrive on real-time insights mined from external data.

This new approach to decision-making moves away from the old paradigm centred on inwardly focused KPIs, financials, annual plans and quarterly reviews.

Instead it analyses external data to understand real-time changes to the competitive landscape. It is an approach that moves the focus away from what you are doing to what the industry is doing. It is an approach that is less concerned with studying the past than with anticipating the future. It is a new decision paradigm that is enabled by the prolific adoption of the internet. It is a new decision paradigm for a new digital reality. At Meltwater we call it Outside Insight.

| | Old Paradigm | New Paradigm |
|---|---|---|
| Focus | My company | My industry |
| Information Sources | Internal | External |
| Analytics | Lagging indicators | Leading indicators |
| Cadence | Quarterly | Real-time |
| Mode of Operation | Reactive | Proactive |

In the Outside Insight paradigm the focus shifts to detecting changes in external factors impacting your business, adjusting your course in real time and measuring the effectiveness of your latest move through competitive benchmarking.

Running a company will move away from obsessing about historical operational data and the five-year master plan for global domination. Instead it will transition into embracing an unpredictable future and making sure that every step you take on your journey is one step closer to your goal. It is an agile approach, paying careful attention to the landscape you are travelling through — side-stepping bumps in the road and acting on opportunities as they come your way.

This may sound a bit like flying by the seats of your pants without a solid plan. I will argue to the contrary. The need for a solid strategy will remain as important as ever. But the rigour is moved from the 'plan' to the effort put into real-time detection of changes to your competitive landscape and the effectiveness of every adjustment you make to your course.

Running a company in the Outside Insight paradigm will increasingly start to look like running a series of A/B tests. You iterate through different initiatives and carefully measure how well each of them performs. You invest more money behind those that work and abandon those that prove to be ineffective. Decisions are fact-based, and the yardstick you use to measure success or failure is simple: are you gaining or losing ground on your competitors?

## Decision-making will change in three key ways

In the Outside Insight paradigm decision-making is different in three key ways. First, it adds forward-looking insights from external data as a critical component in the decision process. Second, decisions happen in real time, responding to critical changes in external factors. Third, companies measure their progress and plan for the future by benchmarking against their competitors.

## 1. External data

According to Statista, an online market research company, the global spend on enterprise software in 2015, excluding spend on hardware and professional services, was $314 billion.[3] Contrast this with research firm Burton-Taylor's estimate that the media intelligence global market in 2014 was worth just $2.6 billion.[4] Admittedly, there's more to external data than media monitoring, but the comparison should still be relevant. Comparing these two research reports, the contrast is startling. For every dollar companies today spend on understanding internal data, about 1 cent is allocated to understanding external data.

Over the last couple of decades enterprise software has helped companies take advantage of the wealth of operational data that companies produce internally. It is time to apply the same rigour in analysing external online data in order to help companies understand the changing dynamics of the world they compete in. By taking external data seriously, a company will get a much better understanding of important external factors and be able to use this to drive strategic decisions that would be impossible based on internal data alone.

Tine, the leading dairy company in Norway, discovered this when a new competitor started to encroach on the market for one of their most lucrative products. For many years Tine had enjoyed over 90 per cent market share in Norway for an iced coffee drink called Tine IsKaffe. Tine was in an enviable position and had created a completely new product category in the Norwegian grocery sector, with strong annual growth. However, in 2010 Tine's market position was challenged when Friele, a distributor of filter coffee and coffee beans, entered the market with a widespread marketing campaign promoting a competing brand of iced coffee.

This came as a complete surprise to Tine. Their management reached out to Meltwater and asked for help in understanding the situation. Tine needed to know how to react to this new threat. What they were in the process of considering when they came to us was a strategic marketing push that would have absorbed significant company resources. Analysing discussions taking place in social media, we were able to identify two key findings.

First, a lot of people were talking about iced coffee online because of Friele's very successful product launch. One of the things that stood out as a strong positive was that people really liked Friele's new, trendy aluminium packaging. This was particularly true of the younger consumers.

Second, people didn't seem to be too excited about the actual taste of Friele's new drink and preferred the iced coffee from Tine. The general consensus online was that Friele's iced coffee was too sweet.

Based on these findings, Tine's managers rejected their initial impulse to launch an expensive advertising campaign and decided instead to take a wait-and-see approach. This turned out to be a good decision. The initial findings on social media held true. In spite of Friele's modern packaging, the actual product didn't manage to threaten Tine's position in the iced coffee segment. Friele was able to enter the market, but was not able to push Tine's market share down below 90 per cent. Friele's entry did, however, cause a boost in the market for iced coffee overall, benefiting Tine, as the dominant player, the most.

Tine's example shows the value that external data – in this case social media – can bring to decision-making. Instead of waiting to see what impact the new competing product from Friele would have on Tine's future sales, a quick analysis identified valuable clues about consumer tastes in product packaging (which would have been hard to get hold of without social media) and helped Tine to choose a measured response to the threat from Friele.

## 2. Real time

External data offers us a real-time view of how our ecosystem and competitive landscape are evolving. Using real-time analytics, we can spot opportunities and threats much earlier than previously and act accordingly. The habit of using the last quarter's set of results in order to set the course for the following quarter does not cut it any more. Instead, external data empowers companies to adjust to events as they unfold.

In 2008 one of the world's largest sportswear brands became aware of a troubling issue through Meltwater's real-time analytics. In the UK its hooded sweatshirts had become associated with criminal activities – police reports published in the media often mentioned suspects using the sportswear brand's hoodies to hide their identity when committing crimes.

The company considered the situation: its brand had been hijacked. The discovery was shared among various departments, who considered how the company should respond. The R&D team took a close look at the exact mechanics of how the clothing was being used by some to shield their faces from their victims and from CCTV cameras. The sweatshirt had originally been designed with a deep hood that projected several centimetres in front of the forehead, making it possible for the wearer to conceal his or her face. The R&D team evaluated possible design changes, finally arriving at a solution that protected their brand and solved the central problem. The new hooded top featured a redesign, so that its front edge could not be pulled far enough forward to mask the face. Once the new hoodies were in the shops, references to the brand declined steadily in UK police reports.

Thanks to real-time analytics, the sportswear giant identified that its brand was being tarnished by criminal activity and quickly found a way to redesign its product to mitigate the problem. Acting swiftly, it was able to address the issue before it blew up and walked away from the incident with no harm to its brand.

## 3. Benchmarking

One of the most fascinating opportunities with external data is that you can learn as much about your competition as you can about your own company. This is an unprecedented opportunity unique to Outside Insight. Outside Insight can help you to analyse your competitors in real time, and through benchmarks you can create great insights into your strengths and weaknesses compared with your peers and answer important questions such as: how many salespeople do you hire compared with the rest of the industry? How often is your brand presented positively in tier 1 media compared with your competitors? And are you investing less or more than the industry average in online advertising?

For this reason I often think of the Outside Insight opportunity as 'benchmark science'. Using external data you can create an 'apples-with-apples' comparison based on third-party data to measure how well you stack up against competition. Such benchmarking creates brutally honest metrics that cut straight through internal bias and misconceptions, and, used appropriately, it can be the deciding factor that tips the scales in your favour.

Hike Messenger is a home-grown Indian messaging app that has been picking a fight with giants such as WhatsApp and Facebook Messenger. Launched in India in 2012, it quickly created a strong following; in January 2016 it announced that it had reached more than 100 million users,[5] and, according to CMO Vidur Vyas, had become the clear second player in India in terms of times spent on it, trailing the market leader, WhatsApp, but well ahead of Facebook Messenger. Central to Hike Messenger's success in its David vs. Goliath fight is a sophisticated use of Outside Insight and clever benchmarking.

Messaging is a very interesting space that has become a fierce battleground for future online dominance. The most sophisticated messaging apps have been developed in Asia, and the leaders of the pack are WeChat (China), Line (Japan) and Kakao (South Korea), which all have grown into fully fledged ecommerce solutions, taxi-hailing apps and mobile money wallets in one integrated app. These apps have demonstrated that messaging apps will become important entry points for online commerce, online content and other online services, a prospect that has started to worry Western online giants such as Facebook, Google and Amazon. How worried became clear in 2014, when Facebook offered $19 billion and a seat on the board to acquire WhatsApp, a company with barely any revenue but which had managed to become the biggest messaging app in the world outside Asia.[6]

| | Launched | Monthly Users | Markets | Services | Market Value $ |
|---|---|---|---|---|---|
| WeChat | January 2011 | 700 million (March 2016) | China | ecommerce, social media, TV, gaming, grocery delivery, taxi hailing, payment | 83.6 billion (Aug 2015) |
| Line | June 2011 | 400 million (June 2014) | Japan | ecommerce, social media, TV, gaming, grocery delivery, taxi hailing, payment | 9 billion (July 2016) |
| Kakao Talk | March 2010 | 170 million (February 2015) | South Korea | ecommerce, social media, TV, gaming, grocery delivery, taxi hailing, payment | 3 billion (March 2015) |
| WhatsApp | January 2010 | 1 billion (January 2016) | Rest of the world | Instant messaging, voice calls | 19 billion (January 2014) |
| Hike | December 2012 | 100 million (January 2016) | India | Instant messaging, voice calls, file-sharing, coupons, games, talking bot, content | 1.4 billion (August 2016) |

**Source:** Statista

India is still a hotly contested market, and, although being the latest player to enter, Hike has been able to steal market share consistently from the dominant WhatsApp and Facebook Messenger by creating unique localized features loved by its users. One such feature is the so-called 'private chat', which can be used to hide who you are chatting with, a feature that is particularly popular among teenagers. 'It all starts with carefully listening to what the consumers want,' Vidur Vyas says. 'Tools like Meltwater are transforming the field of marketing and product development. We use it to understand consumers' needs, to prioritize what product features to invest in, and to design effective marketing campaigns. We use dashboards with real-time competitive benchmarks to understand what works and what doesn't.'

Hike's simple recipe for success has been very

effective. In August 2016, about three and a half years after its launch, it announced a capital raise of US$175 million at a valuation of $1.4 billion.[7] The financing round was led by Tencent, the owner of China's dominating WeChat. Overnight, the local underdog was rolling in cash, and, backed by WeChat's experience in rolling out sophisticated online services, Hike had suddenly become a worthy contender to Mark Zuckerberg for domination of the Indian online market.

# Chapter Five

# The Value of External Data

Internal biases and misconceptions come in all shapes and sizes. We all have them. The inner workings of every company are full of them. Some misconceptions are innocent. Others are very serious. In this chapter we are going to learn about a misconception that cost society trillions of dollars and millions of Americans their homes. It is a strong reminder of how dangerous internal biases and misconceptions can be, and how important it is always to consult external data.

The 2016 Oscar-winning film *The Big Short*, starring Christian Bale, Brad Pitt, Steve Carell and Ryan Gosling, tells the story of four men whose analyses of public data around lending behaviour in 2003–4 enabled them to see what nobody else could see.

Bale played Michael Burry, a hedge fund manager at Scion Capital who predicted the financial crisis as early as 2005. In order to understand how subprime mortgage bonds worked, Burry scanned hundreds, and read dozens, of prospectuses for different mortgage bonds. Each one came with its own 130-page guide, and, according to Lewis, Burry was the only person, aside from the lawyers who drafted them, to read them in detail. Burry used the information to bet against the housing market, earning huge returns for his fund and clients.

By the middle of 2005, over a period in which the broad stock-market index had fallen by 6.84 per cent, Burry's fund was up 242 per cent, and he was turning away investors.[1] By 30 June 2008 any investor who had stuck with Scion Capital from its beginning, on 1 November 2000, had a gain, after fees and expenses, of 489.34 per cent. (The gross gain of the fund had been 726 per cent.) Over the same period the S&P 500 returned just a bit more than 2 per cent.

## The value of external data in correcting insular bias

Burry was making a fortune betting against the housing market. He saw something that nobody else had seen. His secret superpower was simple – he took the time to read the mortgage prospectuses. This was freely available information for everyone to study. It turned out nobody else bothered.

The financial instruments that Burry bet against were known as subprime mortgage-backed securities (MBS) and collateralized debt obligations (CDO). The conventional wisdom was that these instruments were designed by the best risk experts in the industry and in such a way that they could not fail. These instruments were given top AAA credit ratings, so-called 'immune-from-default' ratings, by the rating agencies and became highly sought-after because of their high returns. From 2004 to 2006 the US subprime lending market grew from 8 per cent to 20 per cent of the mortgage market, and it peaked at a staggering $1.3 trillion in March 2007.[2]

Their top credit ratings were based on the assumptions that house prices would rise and that mortgage delinquency would stay at historical levels. When reading the mortgage prospectuses, Burry realized that this was wrong. The demand for subprime instruments had lowered the requirements for who were given mortgages. He discovered an alarming trend in late payments, and he realized that delinquency would go way up compared with historical levels and in the process exert dangerous pressure on house prices.

He realized that the whole world was counting on preconceived beliefs that would not hold true going forward. Everyone was wrong, and the economy was about to come crashing down. He double-checked and triple-checked, but came to the same conclusion every time.

Burry's view was so contrarian at the time that Goldman Sachs had to create a new instrument to make it possible for him to short the market. The notion of shorting AAA mortgage bonds was simply preposterous and had never been done before. In a memorable scene from the film Burry's last ask in his negotiation with Goldman Sachs is for collateral in case Goldman Sachs should become insolvent. Burry genuinely feared that banks could go under and didn't trust the solvency even of Goldman Sachs. Before Burry's predictions came true, he also suffered a massive revolt from his investors, who wanted their money back because they thought he had gone mad.

As we know, Burry's predictions did come true. By October 2007 approximately 16 per cent of subprime adjustable rate mortgages were either ninety days over-due or the lender had begun foreclosure proceedings: roughly triple the rate of 2005. By January 2008 the delinquency rate had risen to 21 per cent, and by May that year it was 25 per cent. Between August 2007 and October 2008 nearly a million US residences com-pleted foreclosure, driving house prices down by nearly 30 per cent.

The subprime crisis in 2007 and 2008 had severe, long-lasting consequences for the US and European economies. The US entered a deep recession, with nearly 9 million jobs lost during 2008 and 2009 – roughly 6 per cent of the workforce. By early November 2008, the US stock market was down 45 per cent from its 2007 high. The crisis would affect everyone. In an article in *Foreign Affairs*, investment banker and former Deputy Secretary of the Treasury in the Clinton administration Roger C. Altman estimates that between June 2007 and November 2008 Americans lost more than a quarter of their net worth.[3]

The crisis in the US also spread to Europe. Several countries, such as Greece, Portugal, Ireland, Spain and Cyprus, were unable to repay or refinance their govern-ment debt or to bail out over-indebted banks and had to seek help from other Eurozone countries, the European Central Bank (ECB) and the International Monetary Fund (IMF). Between 2008 and 2012 Europe also struggled with high unemployment and severe banking losses estimated at €940 billion.[4]

In an 'op-ed' for *The New York Times* on 4 April 2010 Michael Burry, who by now had risen to global fame, argued that anyone who studied the financial markets carefully in 2003, 2004 and 2005 could have recognized the growing risk in the subprime markets.[5] Burry has since said: 'I don't go out looking for good shorts. I'm spending my time looking for good longs. I shorted mortgages because I had to. Every bit of logic I had led me to this trade and I had to do it.'[6]

By analysing publicly available information, Burry discovered a global misconception that would cause one of the largest financial crises in modern history.

## Clearing up the mess

The subprime crisis brought banking giants across the world to their knees. There were genuine fears that the international banking system could collapse, that everyone would lose their money and that the world would tailspin into financial Armageddon.

I didn't understand much of what was going on myself, but I know investment bankers and Harvard graduates who panicked and moved their savings into gold and remote farmland: gold because they feared money would lose its value, and remote farmland to escape social unrest and to grow food. People close to the action were really scared.

Governments around the world had to rescue troubled banks and prevent their economies from collapsing. This happened in the US, UK, Belgium, France, Germany, Iceland, Ireland, Luxembourg and the Netherlands. All over the globe people started to lose confidence in their banks and worry about their savings. As soon as a bank showed a sign of weakness, there was a run on it as people tried to get their money out.

When Northern Rock, the UK's fifth-largest mortgage lender, announced a need for governmental financial support on 14 September 2007, panic broke out and £2 billion, about 10 per cent of the total bank deposits, was withdrawn within forty-eight hours.[7] In one incident police were called to the branch in Cheltenham when two joint account holders barricaded the bank manager into her office after she refused to let them withdraw £1 million from their account.[8] Their money was held in an internet-only account, which they were unable to access after the Northern Rock website crashed owing to the volume of customers trying to log on. On 22 February Northern Rock was taken into state ownership in order to save it from collapse. In the process, all Northern Rock shareholders were wiped out, but Northern Rock customers' deposits were saved.

At the height of the crisis I became concerned about the

health of the US banks myself. To safeguard Meltwater, I instructed all our US funds to be transferred out of the US and out of the US bank system. We wired our excess cash to a bank account we had in the Netherlands. It was not a panic move, but I didn't want to take any risks. A few days later our Dutch bank also announced huge subprime exposures, and this time we moved our money to Norway. My sleepy little home country tucked away in the cold out-skirts of Europe turned out to be one of the safer places to keep money during those uncertain times.

The subprime crisis originated in the US, and it was there that the hurt was most keenly felt. On 3 October 2008 a law was passed in Congress by which $700 billion of emergency liquidity was secured to save US banks from going under.[9] The recipients were all the largest banks in the US, including Fannie Mae, Freddie Mac, Goldman Sachs, Bank of America, JPMorgan Chase, Wells Fargo, Citigroup, Morgan Stanley, Bear Stearns and American Express. The online outlet Propublica.org has developed an excellent feature called the Bailout Tracker, which tracks every dollar and every recipient. In total forty-three banks and insurance companies were saved by the bail-out. Two notable companies, Bear Stearns and AIG, were rescued at the eleventh hour.

Bear Stearns, the eighty-five-year-old investment bank, had famously not laid off a single person during the Great Depression of the 1930s, yet the subprime cri-sis brought the company to its knees. By the end of 2007 it was leveraged at a ratio of 35.6 to 1. On 16 March 2008 the Federal Reserve Bank of New York forced Bear's CEO, Alan Schwartz, to capitulate and sell the company to JPMorgan Chase for $10 per share, a 92.5 per cent discount on the pre-crisis fifty-two-week high.[10] Fourteen thousand employees, who owned around 30 per cent of the shares, lost $20 billion in the deal. But the bank was saved, and they kept their jobs.

AIG, the world's biggest insurer, was deeply entangled in the subprime crisis, insuring a large part of the subprime instruments traded in the US as well as internationally. On 16 September 2008 the unthinkable happened. The eighty-eight-year-old company, trusted around the world for providing protection for individuals and companies, was fighting for its survival and needed protection from bankruptcy. In exchange for $85 billion of taxpayers' money, the US government took a 79 per cent ownership stake in the company.[11] It was a horrible loss for all AIG shareholders, but the alternative was much worse.

| Name | Institution | Amount dispersed (in $) |
| --- | --- | --- |
| Fannie Mae | Government-sponsored enterprise | 116.1 billion |
| Freddie Mac | Government-sponsored enterprise | 71.3 billion |
| AIG | Insurance company | 67.8 billion |
| Bank of America | Bank | 45 billion |
| Citigroup | Bank | 45 billion |
| JPMorgan Chase | Bank | 25 billion |
| Wells Fargo | Bank | 25 billion |
| GMAC (now Ally Financial) | Financial services company | 16.2 billion |
| Goldman Sachs | Bank | 10 billion |
| Morgan Stanley | Bank | 10 billion |

Funds received by top US financial institutions following the 2008 crisis

## *The fall of Lehman Brothers*

One of the most infamous casualties of the subprime crisis was the revered Lehman Brothers. Lehman Brothers was founded in Alabama in 1850 by three siblings who had emigrated from Germany. The bank started out as a commodity trader but grew to become the fourth-largest investment bank in the US, eclipsed only by Goldman Sachs, Morgan Stanley and Merrill Lynch.

For the fiscal year 2007 Lehman Brothers reported record profits of $4.2 billion on revenue of $19.3 billion.[12] A few months later, in September 2008, it was all over for the 158-year-old company, which had weathered two world wars and countless financial crises of the past, such as the railroad bankruptcies of the 1800s, the Great Depression of the 1930s, the Russian debt default of 1998 and the dotcom bubble of 2000. When the subprime crisis brought Lehman down, it employed 26,200 people.

Lehman's collapse was a seminal event that greatly intensified the 2008 crisis. In the month of October 2008, $10 trillion of market capitalization was wiped off global equity markets, the biggest monthly decline on record at the time.

In an excellent piece in *New York* magazine, published in the heat of the global financial meltdown in

November 2008, the writer Steve Fishman scrutinized the then recent collapse of Lehman Brothers.[13] He examined the role of the CEO, Dick Fuld, a man known throughout Wall Street for his ability to intimidate both colleagues and competitors. While the downfall of Lehman Brothers was highly complex, Fishman identifies the fact that Fuld, and other senior executives, were out of touch with the outside world as one of the elements that led to the bank's demise.

On 9 June, close to three months after the collapse of Bear Stearns, Lehman released its second-quarter earnings statement, declaring a $2.8 billion loss.[14] The company assumed that another announcement, one that had been timed to coincide with the earnings statement, would ease the situation. It didn't. Despite announcing that it had secured $6 billion in new investment, Lehman's stock dropped 54 per cent down on the year.

Fishman quotes an unnamed executive at Lehman Brothers who described the mistake as a direct result of the senior management's insular approach. 'The problem was that not many people were dealing with the outside world. Dick [Fuld] didn't talk to [anyone] outside, Joe [Gregory, Lehman President] didn't, the heads of businesses didn't,' the executive is quoted as saying. 'So no one had had a sense of how badly the news would be received.'

'The environment had become so insular,' said another former executive. 'Fuld okayed decisions, but Gregory packaged material so that the choice was obvious. And the executive committee offered no counterweight.'

The misconceptions at the heart of the subprime crisis were catastrophic. The consequences of trusting the toxic subprime instruments ripped through the global banking industry and threatened the existence of almost every bank that people could name. What would have happened if governments across the world hadn't come to the rescue? What would have happened if the banks had gone under and deposits of millions of people and companies had been lost? The consequences would have been devastating: insolvency, bankruptcy and unemployment. The absurdity of the situation is almost hard to fathom.

The root cause of the subprime crisis was the misconception that the sophisticated subprime instruments designed to insulate against risk could not fail. When credit rating agencies such as Standard and Poor's gave their stamp of approval with a Triple A rating, nobody bothered to read the 'fine print'.

The most shameful thing about the financial crisis was that it could have been avoided if people had bothered to read the publicly available information. Burry was the only one who did. The lessons learned from the subprime crisis are many. One key point that stands out is that established biases and misconceptions can be corrected by consulting hard facts and external data.

THE VALUE OF EXTERNAL DATA

*Scan the code using the companion app for more
case studies and video interviews on this topic.
Download at OutsideInsight.com/app.*

*For further reading visit OutsideInsight.com.*

## Chapter Six

# The Value of Real Time

On 12 January 2010 a devastating earthquake hit the Caribbean republic of Haiti — a country with severely limited resources. Within thirty minutes a virtual situation room manned by volunteers across the world began to map information from sources such as social media, email and text. They used an open-source platform called Ushahidi, made in Nairobi, Kenya, that builds products to crowdsource information during crises and periods of political unrest. Collapsed buildings and damaged infrastructure made the situation in Haiti chaotic, but once data was added to the Ushahidi platform, it was possible to gain a clearer view of where resources needed to be focused. For instance, first responders had reports that an orphanage had no drinking water, but they weren't able to locate it in the chaos: Ushahidi researchers were able to map the longitude and latitude of the orphanage and communicate to rescuers the best route to reach it.

This was accomplished because of one important element: real-time data. If first responders had tried to find the orphanage another way — say, via a web search — they would have found only static, historical information. Google Maps, for instance, would not reveal that the earthquake had rendered a road impassable or that a bridge had collapsed. Instead, Ushahidi's crowdsourced mapping and information created dynamic, real-time data that was constantly shifting and offering powerful, practical insights.

Ushahidi, credited with saving thousands of lives, is a Kenyan word meaning 'witness' or 'testimony'. It was created by Nairobian software developer Juliana Rotich, who watched as her city went up in flames during the announcement of the Kenyan general election of December 2007. The hotly contested election results prompted civil unrest, displacing thousands of people from their homes and killing hundreds. On TV there was nothing but soap operas and 1950s' films, because the government had shut down all sources of information. Rotich and her co-founders decided to create a software platform that mapped what was happening, and where, in order to help people stay out of dangerous areas and to guide aid organizations with operational planning and prioritizing their missions. The platform was quickly adapted in areas of crisis elsewhere in the world: initially it was used in African countries such as Kenya, Malawi, Uganda and Zambia, but it has now reached countries in the Middle East, Europe and North America.

The fifth most powerful earthquake ever recorded by a seismograph occurred off the coast of Chile in February 2010 and affected 80 per cent of the population.[1] The earthquake was so powerful that it triggered a tsunami warning in fifty-three countries. It caused significant damage throughout the coastal region of southern and central Chile and as far away as San Diego in California and the Tōhoku region of Japan.

Although he wasn't injured, Sebastián Alegría, a high-school student from Santiago, experienced the devastation, which caused chaos, disorder and food scarcity across Chile. In March 2011 Japan experienced the most powerful earthquake ever to hit that country, triggering tsunami waves over forty metres high. Watching the television news, Sebastián learned that the Japanese have a sophisticated early warning system for earthquakes that is widely distributed throughout the country. Chile had no such system, and Sebastián started to wonder whether he might be able to implement something similar. The obstacles were significant – he wasn't a seismologist or a technologist, he was just a school kid without any resources. How could he possibly hope to achieve something that his own government hadn't been able to do?

Sebastián's solution was ingenious. He bought a domestic earthquake detector for around $75 and replaced the internal circuit with an Arduino – a small, open source microcontroller much like the Raspberry Pi. Both of these credit card-sized computers are loved by hobbyists, who have used them in thousands of home projects. The Arduino interprets the signal from the earthquake detector and passes it on to Sebastián's server, which is connected to Twitter. So, when the detectors pick a signal, instead of sounding an alarm it tweets from an account with the handle @AlarmaSismos that has 442,000 followers.

Here is the type of message it sends out around five to thirty seconds before a perceptible earthquake, depending on the epicentre:

Alarma Sismos @AlarmaSismos <u>27 Apr 2012</u>
Posible sismo durante los próximos segundos en la Región Metropolitana. (Santiago - 14:59:22)[2]

What this means is that 442,000 people in Chile now have access to a detector system for imminent earthquakes in real time on whatever device they're using. Sebastián had an original idea, and technology enabled him to scale it and to make hundreds of thousands of people safer. Since its launch, Alarma Sismos has accurately detected fifty earthquakes.

Public safety was also the prime concern of the Greater Manchester Police when they used real-time social media monitoring to manage and contain riots in August 2011. Following the fatal shooting of Mark Duggan by officers from the Metropolitan Police, thousands of people took to the streets of Britain to protest. Careful monitoring of social media channels to locate looters, source damaged locations and intercept organized activity by riot groups enabled the police to coordinate arrests. It was the first time the British police had used real-time social media in this way.

They monitored Facebook, Twitter, Flickr and YouTube for vital clues and intelligence. Meanwhile, the Twitter feed @gmpolice became the voice of authority

and the real-time source for members of the public looking to find out what was actually happening. Within six
hours of the trouble on the streets, a special 'Most
Wanted' Flickr site had been set up by the Greater Manchester Police featuring photographs of the people they
wanted to arrest.

At its peak, @gmpolice had 101,000 Twitter followers
and more than 7,000 Facebook friends, rising from
1,000. Videos were viewed by over 10,000 people and the
police force's 'Most Wanted' Flickr site had over a million hits. More importantly, public calm was restored
and hundreds of looters were arrested. After the incident
Amanda Coleman, head of corporate communications
at Greater Manchester Police, spoke about the significance of what they had learned during the riots about
external data.[3] 'The events of 9 August were truly life-
changing for communication professionals,' she said.
'Emergency plans that had been largely unchanged for
years are now being torn up and rewritten.'

The Greater Manchester Police, Sebastián Alegría
and Juliana Rotich used technology in an ingenious way
and created solutions with real-time insights unlocking
value for millions of people. Businesses have similar
opportunities if they harness real-time Outside Insights.

In a world where everything happens increasingly
quickly, from shorter innovation pipelines to the speed
with which digital advertising campaigns are launched,
monthly and quarterly backward-looking reviews are
becoming less relevant. Instead of waiting for the effects

of your changing competitive landscape to influence your internal figures weeks or months after the events, you're able to detect shifts in the market-place before they make an impact on your internal results. One company that has taken this opportunity to heart is BHP Billiton.

BHP Billiton is the world's largest mining company and has its headquarters in Melbourne, Australia. Listed in both Australia and Britain, it is one of the world's top producers of iron ore, metallurgical coal, copper and uranium, and has substantial interests in conventional and unconventional oil, gas and coal.

Any enterprise with a global footprint must ensure that information flow to top decision-makers is comprehensive, insightful and timely. It's crucial also for this information to reach key executives quickly and in a coordinated manner, so that everyone is equally and fully informed.

For a company like BHP Billiton, whose industry is the subject of fluctuating global markets and subject to government policy, having succinct, prompt and discerning intelligence is a strategic necessity. Similarly, the very nature of the mining industry means that Outside Insights in the news, for example, are just as likely to come from global financial publications as they are to come from small town freesheets located in the rural areas where BHP Billiton has operations and employees.

To this end, BHP Billiton managers all over the world receive a daily report from Meltwater covering the most relevant information for their business lines, keeping them abreast of developments in their own organization and in those of their competitors, and of changes in energy policy and industry news. We monitor and analyse digital breadcrumbs from many different sources for news. Important information might include opinion on government legislation, competitor movements and investments as well as critical financial and mining news.

This global, streamlined, real-time source of Outside Insight has empowered the company to act more swiftly and efficiently, especially in response to crises. This became critical on 5 November 2015, when a dam burst at the Samarco mine in Brazil, a 50/50 joint venture between BHP and its Brazilian partner, Vale. The tragedy in the mineral-rich south-eastern state of Minas Gerais left 750 people homeless and at least fifteen dead, making it one of the worst mining disasters in Brazil's history.[4]

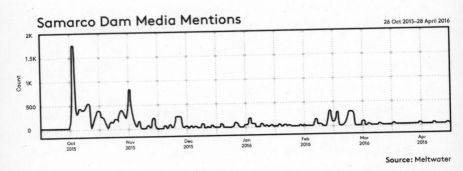

This graph is a vivid depiction of how references in the media to the Samarco dam went from zero in October 2015 to a two-thousand spike on 5 November 2015.

Mariana **BHP Billiton**

# Samarco cent Vale

dams **Brazil** dam burst

water mine people

red mud

**company** disaster accident

Minas Gerais Brazilian mining company

shares **iron ore mine**

**worst environmental disaster**

Source: Meltwater

This word cloud showcases the news articles in 2015 relating to three keywords: dam + Samarco + Brazil. BHP has had a prominent presence in these stories.

During the crisis BHP used Meltwater to monitor, analyse, update and alert the executive management team as the tragedy unfolded. This enabled them to react swiftly and appropriately to the crisis amid a public outcry. For example, *The Guardian* newspaper compared and contrasted BHP's response to events with Vale's, reporting on 10 November 2015 that:

> BHP's public response has been rapid, but Vale, which accounted for more than 10% of Brazil's total exports in 2013, has so far appeared aloof.
>
> BHP chief executive Andrew Mackenzie held a news conference in the hours following the disaster

and the company announced he would travel to Brazil to survey the damage. It has also splashed almost daily updates on the tragedy in English and Portuguese across the top of its website.

By contrast, Vale released a five-sentence statement some 24 hours after the dam collapsed and referred questions to Samarco. Vale's chief executive, Murilo Ferreira, made an unannounced visit to Mariana on Saturday, which the company revealed two days later.[5]

## Minute Maid solves business problems with real-time insight

Coca-Cola's Minute Maid also harnesses the power of real time to solve business problems. In an online Bloomberg article from 2013, executives from Coca-Cola describe how real-time external data is helping the beverages company engineer and standardize 'Mother Nature'.[6]

The brand competes in the $4.6 billion US market for pasteurized juices and real juice products not created using concentrates. These juices are complex to produce – a lot more so than bottled soft drinks – but consumers are willing to pay as much as a 25 per cent premium. Maintaining uniform quality, taste and texture of orange juice when the crop might be coming from Florida, California, Brazil or Israel is a challenge. Add to that variable standards of fruit, labour, transportation, water supply and disease, and one can start to understand how complex a problem Minute Maid is dealing with. For example, in 2014–15 the volume of US orange production was down 350,000 tonnes to 5.8 million because of so-called 'greening disease', a virus spread by the Asian *citrus psyllid*, a type of plant louse that had infested an estimated 70 per cent of citrus trees in Florida.

The situation was thrown into relief when one of Minute Maid's biggest clients – a fast-food company – announced that it intended to shift its business to an orange drink with only a tiny amount of fruit content that, by its very nature (or lack of it) had predictable and stable characteristics.

Minute Maid turned to data, analysing the 600 flavours that comprise the taste of orange – acidity, sweetness and other attributes. The company developed a complex model with a multitude of variables to ensure its products are consistent, predictable and dependable, including expected crop yield derived from detailed satellite images, weather, cost pressures and regional preferences.

Taking this data, Minute Maid worked with an Atlanta-based forecasting and optimization company called Revenue Analytics to create a production model that standardized the production of orange juice. Today the company has a precise formula for how to blend orange juice for a consistent taste and texture (pulp is a significant factor in orange juice production) that takes into account regional tastes. People in Argentina, for instance, have different preferences from those in Massachusetts. Most importantly, the approach is dynamic, adjusting according to external data inputs: if there's a hurricane or an unexpected frost, if there are labour issues or another type of disruption to the supply chain, the entire production process can be realigned and optimized within five to ten minutes.

This is not a secret formula but an algorithm that they call The Black Book. This algorithm determines every aspect of the process, from the optimal time for the oranges to be picked, which is determined according to satellite data, to the exact taste of the beverage that ends up in refrigerators in supermarkets across the world. Every aspect of the product is controlled, meaning that orange juice is no longer subject to the vagaries of nature; instead it's governed by algorithms, precise processes and rigorous real-time analysis.

## Walmart uses real time to predict customer behaviour

The influence of Outside Insight has been significant in every industry, but none more so than retail. Today the industry is an incredibly competitive market-place with online giants stealing market share for little financial margin – the goal is to bring customers inside the business and develop loyalty. Most big box retailers now have consumer apps that offer a direct price comparison: if I visit a Kiddicare store in any small English town, I can look at the brand's app on my smartphone and receive a real-time price comparison with prices on Amazon. And Kiddicare will match whatever price the Seattle-based online retailer is offering at that instant.

Walmart, the biggest retailer in the world, reported revenue of $485 billion for its 2015 fiscal year and employment of 2.2 million people.[7] Walmart handles more than 1 million customer transactions per hour, feeding databases estimated at 2.5 petabytes: 167 times the amount of data to be found in the Library of Congress.[8]

The retailer recently asked Hewlett-Packard to construct a data warehouse capable of storing 4 petabytes (4,000 trillion bytes) of data, representing every single purchase recorded by their point-of-sale terminals (around 267 million transactions per day) at their 6,000 stores worldwide. By applying machine learning to this data, they can detect patterns indicating the effectiveness of their pricing strategies and advertising campaigns, and better manage their inventory and supply chains.

But Walmart doesn't simply analyse real-time internal data; it also looks at real-time external information. For example, close to 100 million keywords are analysed daily to optimize bidding on Google AdWords. This way Walmart is able to measure changing demand for a multitude of products shaping pricing strategies as well as decisions on what stock to hold.

Understanding customers through these various data sources develops practical insight. Big data sets are parsed, sometimes generating singular understandings. When a hurricane is heading towards a certain location, one would expect certain products — torches, candles, bottled water — to gain popularity there. But by combining weather data with Walmart's internal data, the company has made more surprising discoveries. For example, beer sales increase significantly. Again, this may be not so surprising. But the product with the biggest increase in sales is a packaged good that is cheap, non-perishable and easy to store: strawberry Pop-Tarts. Walmart's discovery that sales of these pre-baked pastries increase seven-fold in regions affected by hurricanes has meant that store managers are now requested to place Pop-Tarts near the tills whenever Walmart's real-time analysis discovers a hurricane warning has been issued.

In 2011 Walmart went further, purchasing the data analytics company Kosmix, based in Mountain View, California, for $300 million.[9] The start-up, now called WalmartLab, specializes in aggregating information from social media by topic in real time. Analysing social media, Walmart can now anticipate consumer demand in real time and better manage its vast network of inventory. For a retailer that has 32.7 million Facebook fans and which experiences close to 300,000 social mentions per week, analysis of real-time data streams via social media gives Walmart access to highly individualized consumer insights. If transactional historical (internal) data shows what customers have bought in the past, social networking data has the potential to show what they may buy in the future. In 2011 the team correctly anticipated heightened customer interest in cake pop makers based on social media conversations on Facebook and Twitter. A few months later it noticed growing interest in electric juicers, tied in part to the popularity of the juice-crazy documentary *Fat, Sick and Nearly Dead*.

Boards typically meet quarterly, but consumer retail can change tremendously in three months. Walmart has shown that sophisticated analysis can be used to develop a real-time understanding of consumer demand. Using sophisticated analysis of external as well as internal data, Walmart is able to drive sales, optimize pricing and make better stock decisions.

## Real-time external data creates value for the airline industry

In November 2012 Kaggle, Alaska Airlines and General Electric launched the first phase of what was described as the Flight Quest Challenge, which involved prize money of $250,000.

Kaggle is the world's largest community of data scientists. It organizes competitions in order to solve complex data science problems. One of its projects sought to solve the scourge of modern travellers, a phenomenon that causes the loss of billions of dollars in productivity, not to mention huge amounts of stress for those involved: flight delays.

The purpose of the competition was to use external data to make flying more efficient and to enable pilots to predict with a higher degree of accuracy when a flight might land. Each team was provided with two months of flight data — material such as arrivals, departures, weather and the longitude and latitude of flight.

The competition required teams to design an algorithm that supplied pilots with real-time data on the flight 'profiles', patterns that begin before take-off and end after landing. A typical commercial airliner will have seven phases of flight profile: pre-flight, take-off, departure, en route, descent, approach and landing. Every phase is unique because of factors such as wind speed and the size and power of the aircraft.

Flight profiles are crucial for the air industry. For example, a plane isn't allowed to leave the gate until it has been granted 'clearance delivery', meaning that the flight plan or 'strip' has been approved. This plan is generated in the control tower, which takes into account variables such as other aircraft and the weather.

However, there are multiple factors that can cause a flight to miss its schedule. For instance, a strong headwind will slow down a flight. Pilots then have to ask the flight controller for permission to burn more fuel in order to land the flight on time; this has an impact on the cost index of the flight and requires a process of permissions to be granted. Automating these processes has enormous benefits both for passengers and for the airlines themselves. For example, in 2014 British holidaymakers wasted a total of more than 285,000 hours – or thirty-two years and eight months – owing to flight delays.[10]

The competition called for an algorithm that would make what happens in the air – the way that the profiles are conducted – more efficient, in order to make flight arrivals more accurate.

The winning team, Gxav &*, was announced in March 2013. None of its five members had any experience of the airline industry. They had taken the data from General Electric and used forecasting and predictive modelling software to estimate gate and runway arrival times that were 40 to 45 per cent improvements on the standard industry benchmark estimates. The key was ensuring that optimal decisions were made without delay, which helped airlines reduce congestion at airport gates and manage crews more effectively. This is estimated to save travellers five minutes at the gate, which translates to $1.2 million in annual crew costs and $5 million in fuel savings for a medium-size airline.[11]

The cases discussed in this chapter vary greatly in terms of focus and benefit created. Ushahidi and Sebastián Alegría's earthquake detector are used to save lives. Minute Maid standardized the process of creating a consistent flavour for its orange juice. Walmart predicted customer demands; and the airline industry found ways to save billions of dollars reducing flight delays.

They have one important thing in common and that is that they all harvested the value of real-time analytics. As companies increasingly embrace the importance of Outside Insight and the need to be on top of the constant changes in their competitive landscape, real-time analytics will come to be a fundamental part of every executive's toolbox.

*Scan the code using the companion app for more case studies and video interviews on this topic. Download at OutsideInsight.com/app.*

*For further reading visit OutsideInsight.com.*

# Chapter Seven

# The Value of Benchmarking

In the spring of 2006, when we launched Meltwater in the US with an office in Mountain View, one of our first clients was a local, little-known, start-up in the online video sector with about twenty employees. We didn't really understand what they did and certainly didn't understand their business model. What intrigued us, though, was the way the online video company used our service. The name of the company was YouTube.

They asked us to measure their share of voice in online media, in real time, in order to benchmark their brand against their competition. In 2006 there were a handful of players in the video sector, and it was anyone's guess who would come out on top. Initially every player was mentioned about the same number of times – Vimeo, Dailymotion, Stupidvideos, Break, Google Video, MSN – but then it started to change.

During the early summer of 2006 YouTube started to pull away from its competitors. Momentum grew; it generated more media coverage, thereby strengthening the brand, which in turn attracted more consumers. This was an early indicator that YouTube would rise to the top. On 9 October 2006 it was sold to Google for $1.6 billion.[1] Today the online video-sharing company has become the world's default repository for videos from Keyboard Cat and Dramatic Squirrel to Martin Luther King's 'I Have a Dream' speech. It's all there.

In this particular industry scale is everything, and the winner takes all. By tracking share of voice, YouTube cleverly benchmarked itself against the competition. It would have been hard for YouTube to access user growth and other traction metrics from its competitors. By looking outside and measuring share of voice of online news, YouTube was able to get a third-party objective measure of how successfully it was competing with its peers.

Benchmarking is the most honest measure of success. It doesn't matter how well you're doing in isolation. It is more important to understand how you are doing compared with your competitors. Say you want to increase your customer happiness by 10 per cent. You define new processes, train your people, and after a year of hard work you measure an improvement of 15 per cent. This is a great result, right? But pause for a minute. How do you know if your position has actually improved? What about your competitors? Have they also worked to increase customer satisfaction? If their position has improved more than your own, you are actually worse off than you were a year ago. If they have stood still, then you have improved your position. Without benchmarking against competition, you would not know the true picture.

## Benchmarking methodology

Benchmarking methodology was established by Robert C. Camp, a former executive at DuPont, Mobil Oil and, most recently, Xerox, where he was responsible for best practice in products, services and business processes. Camp defined benchmarking as 'the search for industry best practices that lead to superior performance'.[2]

In the early 1980s, when Camp was at Xerox, high-quality Japanese competitors were rapidly gaining market share and selling their products at the production cost of Xerox products. Camp initiated a project called 'product quality and feature comparisons', which involved the purchase of competitors' products, which were then torn apart and analysed. Xerox learned that key to the Japanese success was a highly efficient manufacturing process, which persuaded the team to move the focus of their investigation to the organizational level of their competitors.

According to Jan-Patrick Cap, from the Global Benchmarking Network (GBN) at Fraunhofer Institute for Production Systems and Design Technology in Berlin, benchmarking – in addition to basic comparison of companies – 'enables the objective monitoring of the competitive landscape to identify best practices that allow the sustainable development of outstanding competitive advantages'.

The practice of benchmarking isn't a new phenomenon: Cap cites Henry Ford's introduction of the assembly line in his automotive plants after watching processes inside a slaughterhouse. Recently there have been significant examples of one industry learning from another: for instance, the introduction of lean principles (taken from Clayton M. Christensen's book *The Innovator's Dilemma*) to reduce errors during surgery, and the McLaren Formula One team establishing McLaren Applied Technologies, which takes its research findings from motor sport and applies them to industry – for instance, working with GlaxoSmithKline to optimize performance at its toothpaste factory near Maidenhead.

Cap argues that benchmarking is successful when data is compiled in a way that is easy to understand so that root causes can be identified and action taken. Modern benchmarking software dashboards enable us to evaluate this information in ways that were previously impossible – more of this in Chapter 13, when I look at the rise of a new software category. But it's clear that any tool that enables an organization to examine itself, the market-place and the competition in an objective way needs to become core to strategic thinking. According to the management consultancy Bain & Company, benchmarking has consistently ranked among the top management tools over the last fifteen years.

'If an organization is not performing benchmarking, it is walking blind through the world and ignoring a significant amount of valuable information,' Cap says. 'If you are not benchmarking, you are looking at a single data point in a world where a single data point has no value. The data point only gains value if you can see it in comparison to other data points and build a relation between them. I do not believe that an organization can exist without benchmarking.'

## Predicting a brand's future strength

A paper from 2015 analysed how online reviews could be used to predict a brand's future strength.[3] Data on seventy-seven consumer electronics and technology brands, such as Apple, Sony and Motorola, was collected between November 2009 and February 2011. Each month the authors monitored 7,376 unique sources (via the media monitoring service Nielsen) from discussion forums to blogs, from social media to media platforms. One of the challenges of monitoring brands on social media is the sheer volume of content that's generated. The paper's authors recognized this, noting that Apple products were mentioned 601 million times in social media in 2013. 'Unfortunately, available data are often noisy, making it difficult to easily extract meaningful marketing insights,' they said.

To their surprise they found that social media sentiment correlated very poorly to a brand's future strength. Only when a brand was analysed in relationship to its competitors could a strong correlation be found between online sentiment and the brand's future strength.

The study concluded that brands don't exist in a vacuum: consumer sentiment about a product cannot be established in isolation, and opinions about other brands will need to be taken into account, as brand strength is established relatively. A consumer might prefer Dodge trucks to those of GM, but would never purchase either as he has a long-standing relationship with Toyota products.

As consumers we are constantly comparing and making decisions based on our preferences – we favour a certain brand of washing-up liquid because it lasts longer, or is more environmentally friendly or is cheaper than another brand. It might not be our ideal product, but we make our choice by comparing and contrasting the options available – we benchmark.

### Posting a different competitive landscape

The power of benchmarking lies in its transparency. It has a brutal honesty. You see your business's place in the world, the truth, warts and all. There's nowhere to hide.

For example, J. D. Power's annual surveys have become one way for the automobile industry to measure itself against competition, with the Initial Quality Study (IQS) measuring problems experienced within the first ninety days of ownership and the Vehicle Dependability Study (VDS) measuring problems experienced after three years of ownership. Similarly, the Department of Transport's on-time arrivals and lost baggage is another external measure for airlines to benchmark themselves.

Many companies have introduced 'best of breed' benchmarking: looking at one industry to compare themselves against the best distribution system, for example, and at another to benchmark against innovation pipelines in order to set their own performance. A *Harvard Business Review* case study tells the story of Commerce Bank, a New Jersey-based retail bank that had a market value of $800 million at the end of 1996 and sold itself a decade later to Toronto-Dominion Bank for $8.5 billion.[4] The bank's leadership team refused to benchmark themselves against other banks like Citigroup but looked at retailers including Starbucks, Target and Best Buy, leading to innovations such as Saturday and Sunday openings.

In contrast, internal data is harder to interpret. It's tough to draw parallels between the different reporting structures and different metrics that department heads and product managers use to prove they have the best department in the business. The naked truth of benchmarked data is one reason why it speaks so loudly to executives in the boardroom.

## *Benchmarking at the USPS*

The US Postal Service (USPS) is an independent government organization that has the rare distinction of being authorized by the constitution. It has America's largest retail network – larger than McDonald's, Starbucks and Walmart put together domestically. In 2014 the service processed 155.4 billion pieces of post – 40 per cent of the world's mail.[5] It's one of the largest employers in America, with 486,822 full-time workers in 31,622 retail locations generating $68.9 billion in revenue for the fiscal year of 2015. The organization lost $5.1 billion in the same year, which is less than the 2014 deficit of $5.5 billion, although the organization faces the challenge of a declining number of people using its core services because of the rise of electronic communication. The company competes with the two giant American global courier companies, UPS and FedEx, as well as the German company DHL. The strength and scale of USPS's network leads both UPS and FedEx to pay the national postal service to deliver more than 470 million of their ground packages to residences.[6]

USPS beats both UPS and FedEx in terms of delivery times and cost, according to research by Stamps.com, with an average delivery time of 1.79 days, compared with UPS's 2.75 days and FedEx's 2.21 days, and an average cost to ship a 2lb. package at $7.34 versus $10.45 for UPS and $10.40 for FedEx. This benchmarking on delivery and price suggests that USPS performs relatively well in terms of delivering a competitive service to its customers.

USPS decided to benchmark its performance compared with its competitors in terms of perception and share of voice. As a government-owned organization and one of the US's largest employers it's important that it maintains a positive image. It is also facing significant business challenges – not only less physical mail, because of the rise of digital communication, but also well-resourced competitors who spend heavily on advertising.

With an operation on such an enormous scale, monitoring media coverage over a sprawling organization is a significant task. Moreover, benchmarking itself against the competition in terms of share of voice and positive and negative sentiment helps USPS get a proper sense of how its employees' behaviour affects the entire organization.

The USPS works with Meltwater to track its mentions in the media, comparing coverage with that of its competitors to understand how the brand is perceived in the market. Analysis showed that USPS in 2015 had 13 per cent share of voice in the US. What's interesting is that, although USPS received less coverage than its competitors, overall it ranked first in media prominence – a measure calculated on potential viewership and how prominently it is presented when it is mentioned. This shows that, although USPS received the least coverage, it did receive the highest-quality coverage.

## Share of Voice Based on PV

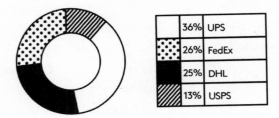

| | | |
|---|---|---|
| | 36% | UPS |
| | 26% | FedEx |
| | 25% | DHL |
| | 13% | USPS |

## Prominence

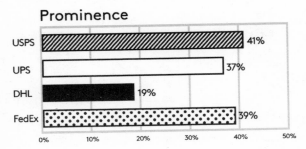

**Source: Meltwater**

Analyses showing USPS benchmarked with competitors.
PV = potential viewership, a figure used to depict how many eyeballs
the company is getting on the stories in which it is mentioned.

Another interesting aspect of the USPS brand story
is that it has significantly more positive sentiment than
its other competitors. This is very evident in a side-by-
side comparison of the four peers for the year of 2014 in
online media. In terms of percentage of total mentions,
each of the players had around 12–13 per cent positive
mentions. When it came to negative mentions, USPS
had about a quarter of the negative mentions that FedEx
had, and about half those of UPS and DHL. For all the

players the negative sentiments were mostly rooted in unhappiness about the promptness and quality of deliveries, showing that USPS was able to hold its own in a competitive space.

## 2014 Sentiment

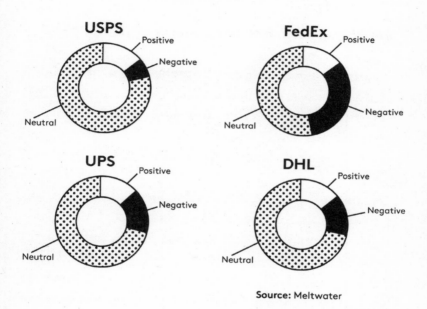

**Source:** Meltwater

Businesses tend to have a narrative about their performance – sometimes these are true and sometimes not. Third-party apples-to-apples benchmarking is an objective and brutally honest measure of a company's performance. For USPS its brand and customer happiness are very important, as most clients don't care much about who does the deliveries of their parcels as long as it is done competitively in terms of price and promptness. USPS analyses show that in terms of visibility the private players are better at getting their brand out there, but when it comes to quality media coverage and client satisfaction, USPS stands up well to the competition.

## Benchmarking: gaining a sense of perspective

In the early 1400s Filippo Brunelleschi, a hot-headed goldsmith with no formal architectural training, rediscovered linear perspective. Linear perspective enables artists to use a single vanishing point to create an illusion of three-dimensional space on a two-dimensional canvas.

Because of its superior realism, Brunelleschi's linear perspective rapidly spread throughout the whole of Italy and then through western Europe. In the same way as Brunelleschi transformed 2D flat views into 3D worlds with depth and life through his linear perspective, so a benchmarked perspective offers a richer and more realistic world-view of a company's strengths and weaknesses. Benchmarking a company with its competitors using external data offers an honest and realistic perspective of the company's place in its competitive landscape.

# THE VALUE OF BENCHMARKING

*Scan the code using the companion app for more case studies and video interviews on this topic. Download at OutsideInsight.com/app.*

*For further reading visit OutsideInsight.com.*

# Part Three

**Outside Insight in Practice**

# Chapter Eight

# Outside Insight for
# Boards and Executives

On Thursday, 22 October 2015, Doug Oberhelman, the chairman and CEO of Caterpillar Inc., the world's biggest construction and mining equipment maker, had disappointing news for Wall Street in his Q3 earnings statement. He reported adjusted earnings of 75 cents per share and revenue of $10.96 billion, missing analysts' expectations of 78 cents and $11.25 billion respectively.[1] He acknowledged the company was going through a 'rough patch' and had to adjust the earnings outlook for the year and sharply increase his estimates on restructuring costs for 2015. 'Our day will come, but it's not right now,' he told CNBC's *Squawk Box*.

One person who was not surprised about Caterpillar's earnings report was Richard Wagner, founder and CEO of Prevedere, a start-up specializing in predictive analytics. 'Early in the year 2015 we did some analysis on Caterpillar and we could see that Q3 2015 was going to be a soft quarter for Caterpillar,' Wagner explains in one of our meetings. Analysing previous results, Wagner and his team discovered that Caterpillar's revenue was highly correlated with external macroeconomic factors such as the price of energy, mining activity and Chinese demand. Taking this into account, they created a forecasting model that would predict a decline in year-on-year revenue for Caterpillar in both the second and third quarter of 2015 owing to unfavourable developments in macroeconomic factors.

**PREVEDERE ECONOMIC RISK REPORT© - CATERPILLAR QUARTERLY YEAR-OVER-YEAR REVEUNE**

*All figures in US$*

| | Q1 2014 | Q2 2014 | Q3 2014 | Q4 2014 | Q1 2015 | Q2 2015 | Q3 2015 |
|---|---|---|---|---|---|---|---|
| **Leading Indicators** | | | | | | | |
| Energy Price Index | ⬇ | ⇧ | ⇧ | ⬇ | ⬇ | ⬇ | ⬆ |
| Coal Shipments | ⬇ | ⬇ | ⬇ | ⬇ | ⬇ | ⬇ | ⬆ |
| Oil Price | ⬇ | ⇧ | ⇧ | ⬇ | ⬇ | ⬇ | ⬇ |
| China Capital Expenditure | ⇧ | ⇧ | ⇧ | ⇧ | ⇧ | ⬇ | ⬇ |
| COMPANY - PREVIOUS YEAR | 13.21 billion | 14.62 billion | 13.42 billion | 14.4 billion | 13.24 billion | 14.15 billion | 13.54 billion |
| ECONOMIC RISK | (596,668,060) ⬇ | (56,318,383) ⬇ | 457,830,511 ⇧ | (212,215,224) ⬇ | (390,422,770) ⬇ | (1,152,917,590) ⬇ | (3,350,219,372) ⬇ |

Source: Prevedere, 2015

Prevedere's analysis shows substantial future pressure on Caterpillar's revenue starting Q4 2014 and gaining momentum through Q3 2015. The net effect of all factors can be seen in the row labelled 'economic risk'.

Studying Prevedere's model, one can see that the negative pressure from the macroeconomic climate had already started in Q4 2014 and gained momentum as the year progressed. For the third quarter of 2015 Prevedere's model quantified the negative pressure to be in the order of $3 billion, pushing Caterpillar below Wall Street's expectations.

Caterpillar sadly never benefited from Wagner's analysis, because he kept it to himself at the time. It was early days for Wagner's start-up, and they used the Caterpillar case to validate their model. Since then, however, Wagner has proved his forecasting model with a number of Fortune 1000 companies, such as Nationwide Insurance,

BMW Financial Services, Hershey, Hamilton Capital Management, Wendy's, Masonite and Yum! Brands. Wagner's start-up helped these companies incorporate external factors in their financial forecasting model and claims to have achieved an average reduction in forecasting error of 50 per cent.

Wagner points to a study from KPMG showing that 60 per cent of companies do not include external drivers of business performance in their financial forecasting models.[2] The same report found that quarterly forecasts among US-listed companies are off the mark by 13 per cent, representing close to $200 billion in lost revenue per year. Wagner argues that this is because most companies exclusively rely on internal performance data. They ignore all the external factors that impact their business. Unknown external factors, from volatility in Asian markets and currency fluctuations to the cost of energy, consumer confidence and changing weather patterns, make it tough for businesses to predict future performance. 'They are essentially doing guesswork in the dark,' Wagner says, and he continues: 'Unless they start to actively incorporate external data into their forecast models they will continue to miss their numbers.'

Wagner is not the only one with this point of view. Doug Laney, VP and distinguished analyst for Gartner Research, who is credited as one of the people who defined the term 'big data', says: 'I've been advising organizations regularly that they need to stop navel-gazing at their own data and realize that there is external data out there that can provide them [with] some significant predictive, prescriptive and even operational benefit.'

In 2015 Laney conducted a study examining the financial indicators of companies that were identified as approaching external data in an information-centric way. They might have a chief data officer, a robust data science programme or any other initiative that suggested they were serious about collecting, managing, deploying and valuing outside information as an asset in parallel importance to internal data on traditional balance sheets. 'Every company talks about information as an asset, but not many companies actually behave that way,' Laney says. 'We looked for companies with these kinds of indicators and then examined their financials.' The study then applied Tobin's Q, a metric devised by the economist James Tobin in 1969, and a simple ratio of market value to replacement value of tangible assets. Laney discovered a significant difference between those companies with and those without a robust and coherent strategy for external data. Organizations that did embrace external data had a market value indicator that was 200 to 300 per cent higher than those with less cultural and financial outlay on data.

## Outside Insight in practice

As the Caterpillar case illustrates, external economic factors can have a huge influence on a company's future performance. It is surprising, therefore, to see that KPMG's research shows that a majority of companies don't look at external data but rely exclusively on internal business drivers when creating their forecasts. Laney's research also shows that those companies that embrace external data create superior valuations to those who don't.

The place to start with embracing Outside Insight is, in my opinion, at the board level and among the executives. Decisions made at this level are the most important in the whole company, determining future successes and failures. To make such critical decisions a big-picture understanding of the changing competitive landscape is important and an intimate understanding of external factors driving future performance a necessity.

In this chapter I propose a simple framework for incorporating Outside Insight systematically into board- and executive-level decision processes. Outside Insight is in its infancy, and as new technology develops over time, the use of Outside Insight by boards and executives will increase in sophistication. I have tried to create a framework that is both sufficiently specific to be useful today and generic enough to be applicable in the long run. The framework consists of three phases, of progressively increasing complexity; each phase comes with a straightforward three-step process.

Phase A in this framework focuses on understanding how the ebbs and flows of your competitive landscape will impact your business. The starting-point here is to understand which external factors your business is most exposed to. Using Outside Insight, these are tracked in real time, creating an early warning system flagging opportunities as well as threats.

Phase B incorporates Outside Insight into fundamental processes such as articulation of strategy and creation of forecasting models, and as a critical feedback loop for measuring the effectiveness of execution.

Phase C is full conversion to the Outside Insight paradigm. In this phase Outside Insight trumps the importance of internal financials. Company objectives, accomplishments and company health are seen through the lens of Outside Insight. In this phase data science, game theory and artificial intelligence (AI) have arrived as central management tools.

## Phase A: Understanding the competitive landscape through Outside Insight

The first phase is all about bringing external information into the boardroom. Any company is impacted by external factors, and the objective in this phase is to arrive at an understanding of which of these have the biggest impact on future performance. By systematically tracking such leading indicators, executives and board will have a better command of their business and will be better equipped to make good decisions.

Step 1 (hereafter called step A1, for clarity) in this

process is to consider external industry-wide factors such as macroeconomic trends. Some of these may be obvious, such as the cost of energy in the case of Caterpillar. A more subtle example, taken from Chapter 6, is weather conditions in the case of Minute Maid, impacting its future supply of oranges.

Analysing the impact of the broad set of external factors can seem like a daunting task. I believe a pragmatic approach can go a long way. In most cases the 80:20 rule applies: 20 per cent of the factors contribute 80 per cent to the value. For most companies it is a big win just to bring external factors systematically into their decision processes. My recommendation is therefore to start in a simple manner and trust intuition. Normally, the company's executive team will have a good sense of what external factors are important to keep an eye on. Vetting suitable candidates by analysing their effect on historical company results should reveal which factors are the most important to stay on top of.

A more rigorous approach would be to use regression analysis or machine learning. This could discover non-intuitive causalities and surprising insights. However, such an approach is a much bigger undertaking and would need specialized expertise in order to arrive at the right conclusions. Unless a company has this expertise in-house, my recommendation would be to wait until after the benefits of the most obvious external factors have been captured.

In step A2 we identify external drivers stemming

from competitive tension. Examples of this can be marketing spend and customer satisfaction. Choosing what to track in step A2 is very similar to the process in step A1. Again the choice is between a pragmatic and a rigorous approach. I favour the pragmatic approach for the same reason as under step A1.

A new element to consider in step A2 is the design of suitable measurements. Economic drivers such as energy costs are easy to track because this is a figure that is publicly available. Areas of competitive tension are much harder to quantify. Take, for example, client satisfaction. How should it be defined? Should it be judged on customer feedback, net promoter score, customer loyalty or maybe 'churn' – i.e., lost clients over a given time period? No perfect definition of client satisfaction exists. The difficulty here is also that whatever definition we choose will require retrieval of the same data across our peer group. Knowing that our customer satisfaction has improved is positive, but without knowing how our competitors' customer satisfaction has developed we won't know whether we have gained or lost ground.

My advice would be to start by selecting an online data type that contains the signal we are looking for. For client satisfaction, social media are an obvious candidate. By comparing your client's social media sentiments with those of your competitors, you will get an objective measurement of how the relative client satisfaction has developed over time.

In step A3 we combine the results of steps A1 and A2

to create an early warning system. Trend analysis should be shared through an online dashboard or included as part of the standard board pack. Abrupt changes to any of the key drivers should trigger instant alerts to executives and board members.

Such a constant flow of Outside Insight provides valuable context for company financials and other internal reports and analyses. This empowers executives and board members to understand important market developments and key challenges ahead properly. Outside Insight also provides a critical correction to internal biases. Are the internal narratives supported by the story we find in the external data? Does management understand where the market is going? Does the existing strategy make sense in light of current market developments?

An understanding of the external factors impacting a company can also be used to create a third-party measure of a company's competitiveness: its competitive health. For example, the strength of a company's brand can be measured as the size of its online footprint in news and social media. By measuring the size of the footprint for all the companies in your peer group, you can measure each company's share of the industry's footprint. For brands this is often called share of voice.

Below is a competitive health matrix illustrating the four different situations a company can find itself in. The competitive health matrix is used to assess the development of a company's competitiveness over a period of time: for example, last month. The X-axis describes the change in the company's online footprint. The Y-axis describes the change in its share of voice (SOV). If both are positive, the company is in the 'Winning' quadrant.

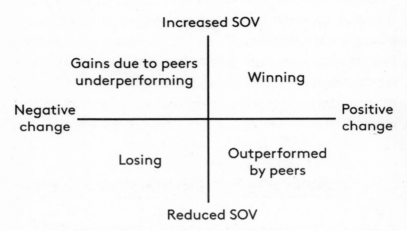

The Meltwater Competitive Health Matrix analyses the change over a certain time period to indicate whether you have gained or lost ground.

Conventional analysis only looks at changes along the X-axis. In the Outside Insight approach changes on the X-axis are irrelevant. The changes that are important are those on the Y-axis. Any positive change relative to your peers is good; any negative change is a set-back. In a dynamic, competitive market progress is a relative measure, quantified in terms of how much you improve compared with your competition.

Completing Phase A of our Outside Insight framework brings an industry perspective created by third-party data into all discussions in the boardroom. The external environment is tracked and analysed in real time, ensuring a proactive, forward-looking mindset. The systematic utilization of Outside Insight provides a real-time score of the company's competitive health and an early warning system that makes it easier to discover new threats – as well as opportunities. A boardroom supported by Outside Insight is more proactive and makes more informed decisions than boardrooms that are not.

| | Description | Explanation |
|---|---|---|
| Step A1 | Identify industry-wide factors such as macroeconomic trends impacting future performance. | Cost of energy, consumer confidence and cost of raw materials. |
| Step A2 | Identify key external business drivers stemming from competitive tension areas that impact future performance. | Marketing spend, customer satisfaction and innovation pipeline. |
| Step A3 | Create an early warning system flagging threats and opportunities. | Dashboards with real-time analysis of drivers found in A1 and A2 - abrupt changes trigger instant alarms. Your competitive health is tracked by real-time competitive benchmarks and the competitive health matrix. |

Phase A: Understanding the competitive landscape through Outside Insight

Edgewell Personal Care is a company that has embraced the importance of Outside Insight and understood the benefit of continuously tracking changes in its competitive landscape. Edgewell is a consumer packaged goods company that owns brands including Wilkinson Sword razors, Hawaiian Tropic suncare products, feminine care brands such as Playtex and Carefree and the skincare brand Wet Ones. It employs around 6,000 people and operates in fifty countries.

The company operates in a highly competitive sector against much larger multinationals, which have greater resources and marketing budgets to match. One way the company keeps an edge is via the flow of information. Paul Pacileo, the manager of commercial planning and strategy at Edgewell, uses Meltwater software to produce a report twice a week that pulls together all the pieces of external data that might impact Edgewell's products.

Pacileo's challenge is to determine what information is relevant to the organization from the deluge of industry data generated every day. To do this he has devised a series of sophisticated, real-time searches for each line of Edgewell's business that create trigger points for external data related to the company's products. He has focused on two areas: first, strategic information related to product lines, such as new products coming to market, product enhancements and news within the competitive set; and second, tactical data such as which products have been placed on sale, developments at major retailers like Walmart and Target, and discounting programmes. A third data stream looks at corporate news about competitors: for instance, cost-saving initiatives, acquisitions and sales of brands.

Pacileo says: 'We look at the forecast without getting too heavy in the financial analysis. If we can understand why a product's sales are either up or down, that's more important: we're interested in why it happened and we'll distribute that to our subscribers throughout the organization.'

Pacileo receives around two hundred data points per day. 'Part of my responsibility is commercial processes, and one of the key focuses or concepts that we use is the idea of a "single point of truth",' Pacileo says. 'We try to centralize the information so that whoever is using it is seeing the same exact thing, so that we're not working in silos. We try to be conscious with revision controls, so that person A is looking at one revision, and person B has a different revision, and they go off and do their thing and then all of a sudden we have a disconnect or a misalign in our strategy.'

Third-party data supports Pacileo in ensuring that the information that he's directing throughout the business enables early decisions to be made by responding to shifts in the market or news stories that require a rejoinder or some form of counter-intelligence. 'If we have a better sense of what the competition is doing and we can get a pulse on that, we are better able to respond and react to situations,' Pacileo says. 'And we're able to be more strategic, because if we can see trends and how things are progressing, based on what resources we have available, we take a calculated risk – but a risk that is well investigated. We're not trying to follow what the competition is doing.'

'We want to know what the competition is doing because we want to measure their effectiveness,' he says.

> If they're doing something that is going to cause us to lose share, well, we better make damn sure that we try to do something to prevent that from happening. At the same time, if they're throwing a lot of money at a programme and the consumption data and the performance data are not indicating a shift, or the category is flat, maybe it's opportune for us to do something . . . Being Edgewell, we don't have the horsepower, we don't have the resources like some of our competitors do, so we have to use different resources. And one of them is knowledge – having a fuller awareness of what's going on in this world. Increase the sense of what our surroundings are in the business world; increase our sense of who our retailers are and try to leverage that as an advantage to create stronger partnerships.

Edgewell's commitment to staying on top of external information is admirable. Their approach is pragmatic, but very systematic. Embracing Outside Insight, they create a deep awareness of their competitive landscape and use this to successfully take on larger and more resourceful competitors in their industry.

## Phase B: Integration of Outside Insight into core internal processes

In Phase B Outside Insight is operationalized by being integrated into core internal processes. The three steps of this phase address strategy, forecasting and how to measure success.

In Phase A we discussed the value of external drivers stemming from competitive tension. In Phase B this concept is taken a step further. The reason for this is that leading performance indicators are not all created equal. Some might help in creating short-term gains, such as temporarily increasing sales, while others are crucial for long-term success.

This is where the importance of strategy comes in. 'Strategy' comes from the Greek word *stratēgia* – the art of the military general. It is a high-level plan created to achieve one or more goals under conditions of uncertainty. The best strategies choose a differentiated market position by harnessing a unique skill.

Step B1 consists of articulating the company strategy in terms of a choice of arena(s) of competitive tension to dominate in order to win against the competition in the long run. A simple example of this could be: 'We will become the winner in our industry by offering the industry's best client support.' Such a choice should be informed by studying the preferences of the desired clients and matching those with an honest but aspirational look at internal capabilities.

The benefit of articulating the strategy in terms of competitive arenas is that such an approach lends itself well to creating an overarching objective against which the company's performance can be measured, using objective external data. By using Outside Insight to design appropriate competitive benchmarks, the success of a company's strategic pursuit can be measured and tracked in real time.

The real-time feedback loop on how successful a company is in its strategic pursuit is very valuable for countering the rapidly increasing pace of change that many industries experience today. If market situations change abruptly, a strategy can be reassessed and adjusted with an Outside Insight approach without losing valuable time.

In September 2012 the *Harvard Business Review* revealed that nearly 90 per cent of executives develop strategic plans on an annual basis, regardless of the actual pace of change in their business environments.[3] The same article outlined a Boston Consulting Group survey of 120 companies around the world in ten major industry sectors, which showed that executives are well aware of the need to match their strategy-making processes to the specific demands of their competitive environments. Still, the survey found, in practice many rely instead on approaches that are better suited to predictable, stable environments, even when their own environments are known to be highly volatile or mutable. The *HBR* article was aptly titled 'Your Strategy Needs a Strategy'. Using Outside Insight, the main challenges pointed out by this article can be addressed.

Step B2 in operationalizing Outside Insight is to incorporate key external drivers into the forecasting model. The purpose of this is to make sure that the forecasts reflect the external factors impacting the business instead of relying on internal data alone.

Such an undertaking requires sophistication in statistics and data science. Some companies have developed this expertise internally. Those who have not can utilize a number of external consultancies. In either case, my advice is to avoid creating models that become too complex. There are a lot of factors determining a company's future performance. When applying data science wizardry, the models tend to become complicated and hard to understand. Avoid ending up with a black box. These are hard to challenge and can cause huge mistakes when they start to go wrong. My advice would be to make the models as simple as possible and to vet them thoroughly, using common sense.

Incorporating Outside Insight into a company's forecasting model will create more reliable forecasts because they are not limited to internal factors. This greater precision will alleviate internal stress, free up executives' time and energy, and allow deployment of company resources more effectively.

Take the case of another company that Prevedere's Wagner worked with, a global beverage producer with products that have an expiry date. When they entered the Chinese market, they started working with distributors for regional markets. It was clear that many of the sales forecasts were being done on gut instinct – accuracy was around 70 per cent, meaning that there was a 30 per cent error even in major Chinese cities.

In the beverage industry, over-stocking is common practice, as brands don't want to hand over shelf space to competitors. Prevedere took large tranches of third-party Chinese government data relating to employment, household income, expenditure, demographics and regional retail sales. The stakes were high. For every percentage point improvement in forecast accuracy, the beverage company was able to reduce shelf stock in its inventory. Examining third-party, external data enabled the beverage manufacturer to increase the accuracy of its forecasting by more than 15 per cent, a saving of millions of dollars.

In step B3 we turn our attention to measuring success or, to put it another way, the effectiveness of a company's execution. With measurable external factors incorporated in both strategy and forecasts, we have created clarity in terms of what it takes to win and an understanding of how external factors translate to future financial performance. This enables the creation of a new set of performance metrics to track how successfully a company is working towards its strategic objectives.

The creation of this new set of performance metrics is rooted in two important tenets of Outside Insight. The first is that improvements are measured in gains with respect to competition. The second is that the most valuable metrics are forward-looking in nature and leading indicators of future performance. This approach is very different from the conventional approach of assessing a company's performance. A financial report from any listed company is quick to state revenue numbers, profit, cash flows and year-on-year growth. Looking at the company through the Outside Insight lens, such information is incomplete. Revenue and profits are historical metrics, and year-on-year growth doesn't contain information about whether the company has gained or lost ground in the last quarter.

I don't want to imply by this that nobody today cares about market share or other measures of relative success. Forward-looking information is also something that the market is clearly very sensitive to. Nor am I saying that financial metrics are irrelevant. What I want to point out is how Outside Insight can be used to create a new set of performance metrics. This third-party data set doesn't wait for quarterly updates but can tell in real time the story of how the industry players are faring in relation to each other. A focus on historical performance metrics such as financials can make executives too internally focused and too short-sighted. Taking advantage of Outside Insight performance metrics can help to ensure a focus on the wider industry development and to position the company for long-term sustainable success.

| | Description | Explanation |
|---|---|---|
| Step **B1** | Articulate company strategy in terms of arenas of competitive tension to dominate. | Example: 'We will become the winner in our industry by offering the best client support.' Creates an overarching objective that the company can use as a yardstick to assess the success of its strategic pursuit in real time. |
| Step **B2** | Incorporate external factors into financial forecasting models. | Sharpens the early warning system from phase A to accurately understand each external factor's contribution to future performance and weigh its importance accordingly. |
| Step **B3** | Measure effectiveness of execution through competitive benchmarking of external leading performance indicators. | Creates a new set of performance metrics complementary to conventional financial metrics. |

Phase B: Integration of Outside Insight into core internal processes

Completing Phase B of the Outside Insight framework, we have moved from an early warning system to a comprehensive operationalization of the value found in external information. A company's pursuit of strategic objectives can be measured in real time using benchmarks describing strategic arenas of competitive tension. This makes it easier to adjust the course if fundamental market assumptions change.

The clarity of a strategy articulated in terms of competitive benchmarks has the added advantage of helping employees understand how their individual work contributes to the whole. The incorporation of external factors into the forecasting model will offer an intimate understanding of the impact that changes in the competitive landscape have on future results. The full potential of external data is utilized when Outside Insight is used to measure the effectiveness of company execution. Simply put, any initiative that improves an important competitive benchmark puts the company in a better position and warrants further investment. Any activity that doesn't should be abandoned. Such an approach offers a view of a company's performance that is complementary to the traditional financials. It secures a focus on broader industry development and optimal allocation of company resources for long-term gains.

## Phase C: Conversion to the Outside Insight paradigm

The third and final phase of deploying Outside Insight represents a fundamentally new approach to business. Financial results are no longer centre-stage and are instead viewed as lagging consequences of historical rankings in competitive benchmarks.

Phase C requires a cultural shift away from the historical focus on internal data, financials and past events.

Annual objectives are no longer expressed in terms of financial goals. Company health is no longer assessed through its profit or cash flow.

A company fully converted to the Outside Insight paradigm is scrutinized through the lens of leading performance indicators found in external data. Success is measured on a relative scale and as a function of how well the company performs according to key competitive benchmarks.

This may on the surface sound radical but, looking around us, we can see that this way of thinking is already starting to take root. The market value of a public company is already more sensitive to management forecasts than to its historic financials. When news breaks about a listed company, its competitors' share prices can rise or fall as a consequence even while their underlying metrics stay static.

Silicon Valley is an early adopter when it comes to embracing the importance of external forward-looking indicators. How often do you hear about a Silicon Valley start-up with zero revenue and a crazy valuation? Is this because Silicon Valley investors don't know what they are doing, or is it because they value a company's worth beyond financials?

In Chapter 3 we saw how Instagram, with its lack of revenue and thirteen employees, was valued at $1 billion by Facebook only eighteen months after launch. Similarly, YouTube was sold in 2006 for $1.65 billion to Google despite having no revenue. Both these examples demonstrate how Silicon Valley is already judging company value in terms of leading performance indicators instead of historic financials.

Mark Zuckerberg valued Instagram at $1 billion because of its momentum in user growth and its leading market position in online photo-sharing. Four years on, financial analysts say the acquisition was a 'steal'. Similarly, Credit Suisse analyst Stephen Ju estimated YouTube's 2015 revenues as $6 billion, representing 8 per cent of Google's total income, and making it one of its fastest-growing revenue streams.[4] Using Google's market value over revenue as a basis estimates YouTube's current value to be approximately $50 billion, making YouTube one of the best acquisitions Google has ever made.

Phase C of deploying Outside Insight does not advocate throwing out 'old school' financials such as profit or cash flow, but is about embracing the significance of today's rankings in competitive benchmarks for future creation of value. The tales of YouTube and Instagram demonstrate that this value will eventually be harvested through generation of hard cash and measured in revenue and profit margins. But that doesn't happen before the battle for top rankings in competitive benchmarks is won.

The last element introduced in Phase C is the use of sophisticated simulation software to aid strategic decision-making. The software runs scenario analysis building on external and internal information. By applying machine learning and game theory, it simulates the outcome of different strategies. Some companies have already started to give intelligent software a vote in final decision-making. The Japanese venture capital firm Deep Knowledge famously appointed an AI to its board, giving it equal weight to other board members. IBM is developing a version of Watson (famous for beating contestants on *Jeopardy*) for the same purpose. With the assistance of sophisticated AI, boards can make more sense of the large quantity of information they have at their disposal about the markets, customers and competitors. AI software can perform complex scenario analyses, which is hard for people to do, and free up humans to focus on what they do best – asking the right questions, using their judgement and inspiring other people – while robots attend to the diagnostics and modelling.

I believe that AI will prove very valuable in corporate decision-making and help boards to make sense of a complex and increasingly fast-paced world as well as facilitating informed and robust data-driven decisions to the benefit of shareholders, employees, clients and other stakeholders.

| | Description | Examples |
|---|---|---|
| Step **C1** | Express annual objectives in terms of leading performance indicators instead of financial goals. | We will improve customer satisfaction compared with our nearest competitor by 5 per cent. |
| Step **C2** | Assess the health of a company in terms of how well it ranks on key competitive benchmarks rather than financials. | |
| Step **C3** | Deploy a rigorous AI for computer-aided decision-making, taking advantage of sophisticated scenario analysis and game theory. | |

Phase C: Conversion to the Outside Insight paradigm

The Outside Insight paradigm will change the way boardrooms are run and companies governed. The framework presented in this chapter describes a step-by-step approach for executives and boards that want to take advantage of the value of external data and Outside Insight in decision-making, goal-setting, forecasting and measuring effectiveness of execution. A full conversion to the Outside Insight paradigm represents a radical shift away from the conventional focus on financials and operational efficiency and towards prioritizing an in-depth understanding of competitive dynamics and leading performance indicators.

In the next chapters we will look in more detail at how Outside Insight can be used in practice to support other functions, such as marketing, product development, risk assessment and investments. The chapters that follow are not framework-based but instead look at how innovative companies use external information and Outside Insight to excel at what they do. The hope is that these examples will inspire the readers to come up with new and innovative ways to put Outside Insight to good practical use in their daily routine, whether they work in one of those described functions or not.

*Scan the code using the companion app for more case studies and video interviews on this topic. Download at OutsideInsight.com/app.*

*For further reading visit OutsideInsight.com.*

## Chapter Nine

# Outside Insight for Marketers

According to Wikipedia, the *Guinness Book of World Records* is the best-selling copyrighted book of all time.[1] The idea for the book grew out of an argument that Sir Hugh Beaver, the managing director of Guinness Breweries, had after a shooting party where he missed a shot at a golden plover. The disagreement that erupted was regarding which game bird was the fastest in Europe: the golden plover or the red grouse. Beaver realized that there was no book where this information could be found, and that every day there must be countless similar disagreements in pubs across the world where a final settlement of the discussion cannot be found in any book. And that is how the annual tradition of the *Guinness Book of World Records* started. The 2017 edition marks its sixty-third consecutive year of publication.

During these sixty-three years the world has changed, and today we have access to the world's consolidated knowledge at our fingertips. I constantly find myself searching Google for trivia. What is the population of Ethiopia? (The answer is 94.1 million; it overtook Egypt in 2000.[2]) What is the length of the Norwegian coastline? (The answer is 25,148 km, comprising 2,650 km of mainland as well as long fjords, numerous small islands and minor indentations of 22,498 km.[3])

When I search for 'the fastest game bird in Europe', I learn that the golden plover is the correct answer. When searching for the 'fastest game bird in the world', I discover that the teal has the highest top speed (88 m.p.h.).[4] The snipe, however, is harder to shoot from shooting range, whereas the teal is easier to hunt because it accelerates more slowly.

The online consolidation of the world's knowledge is not only changing our access to trivia such as the flight speed of game birds. It also gives us an unprecedented opportunity to research the pros and cons of any product we are thinking of buying. We do our research online and make the purchase decision based on what the research tells us. This trend has transformed marketing over the last twenty years more than any other. Consumers' purchase decisions used to be highly susceptible to marketing. Today traditional marketing techniques have become much less effective because consumers turn to online research before making up their mind. They don't trust marketing. They are looking for what other people are saying about you – they are looking for social proof.

## *Three fundamental changes affecting marketing*

Marketing has been transformed dramatically during the last twenty years as a consequence of the new digital reality described in the first part of this book. A lot has been written about how marketing has changed. There is no shortage of experts, books and blogs about the subject. In simple terms, I will argue that all this literature describes the consequences of three fundamental changes that have taken place, each transformative in itself.

The first big change is that in our new digital reality everything has become measurable. Every single campaign or user engagement can be rigorously analysed. In the process, marketing has moved from being a predominantly creative discipline where return on investment (ROI) was often vague and hard to calculate, to a number-crunching exercise optimizing ROI by analysing page impressions, click-through rates and user engagement in real time.

The second change is the introduction of social media. Social media represent a completely new era for market research, providing an unprecedented opportunity to learn about the needs and preferences of your target clients. For the first time in history companies can have direct access to people's hearts and minds. Unsolicited and in real time, they can listen in to people's conversations about their product and how it compares to that of competitors.

The third change is that the process through which people make a purchase decision has been turned upside down. The time when companies could rely on marketing campaigns pushed at target clients is over. Today the information flow has moved from push to pull. Before making any decisions, people research your reputation online. They are looking for evidence that they can trust you and your brand.

Internalizing these three transformative changes lies at the heart of crafting a successful marketing strategy today. Marketers need to build a technically savvy organization to analyse and optimize the performance of their campaigns. They need to design a strong programme for mining social media in order to stay on top of their target customers' shifting likes and dislikes. Their actual marketing effort should focus on promoting social proofs and other favourable online breadcrumbs so that they can more easily be found in the research carried out by their target customers.

## From black magic to number-crunching

The famed Philadelphia merchant and marketing pioneer John Wanamaker (1838–1922) is credited with innovations such as the 'price-tag' (prices even in department stores used not to be fixed but were negotiable) and 'money-back guarantee'. His most famous legacy, though, is the oft-quoted remark 'Half the money I spend on advertising is wasted; the trouble is I don't know which half.'

For many years that was the trouble with marketing. There was no feedback loop to measure the specific impact of marketing campaigns. All of this changed with the internet. On the internet everything could be tracked and measured: for instance, how many times an ad was shown and how many times it was clicked on. The click stream could be tracked all the way to the point where the purchase decision was made or to the point where it was rejected.

In the process marketing has been transformed from an industry of creative types to one of number-crunchers. An excellent illustration of this is Barack Obama's bid to be re-elected President of the USA in 2012. His 2008 presidential election win came at the back of one of the first successful political campaigns on social media. For his re-election, Obama successfully doubled down on the success he had had with social media from 2008, and created a data-driven campaign that would be heralded by marketers for years to come.

Central to Obama's new campaign was Dan Wagner, who was hired in January 2009 as National Targeting Director of the Democratic National Committee (DNC), the governing organization of the Democratic Party in the USA. His job, in layman's terms, was to identify people who might vote for Barack Obama and persuade them to turn out on the day.

Typically, voter research had been conducted by

taking small samples of voter data and then treating this information as representative of sentiment on a larger scale. Wagner had an entirely different approach, one that embraced the new digital reality. Wagner's approach was one of the first large-scale examples of how powerful Outside Insight can be if used correctly. According to the *MIT Technology Review*,

> His techniques marked the fulfilment of a new way of thinking, a decade in the making, in which voters were no longer trapped in old political geographies or tethered to traditional demographic categories, such as age or gender [...] Instead, the electorate could be seen as a collection of individual citizens who could each be measured and assessed on their own terms.[5]

A single massive data depository was created that could merge the information from fieldworkers, consumer databases and pollsters and marry that with newer information such as Facebook accounts, Twitter handles and mobile numbers. The system also enabled campaigns to run tests in which two versions of a message were sent to see which one performed better. It turned out that the better-performing messages were around ten times as effective as the ones that performed poorly. The team discovered that voters seemed to be most receptive to messages from Michelle Obama. Joe Biden? Not so much.

Wagner's team discovered that half of the campaign's

target voters in the 18–29 demographic were completely unreachable by phone. But analysis of social media provided a crucial and powerful insight. Of all Facebook users in the US, 98 per cent had a friend who was a fan of Obama. The campaign recognized that the world had speeded up. Voters were used to mobile apps that removed friction and made their lives simpler. Based on this, the team built an app that was downloaded by 1.2 million Obama fans in the younger demographics. The campaign used this app to mobilize Obama supporters in swing states to encourage their Facebook friends to vote for Obama. The campaign found that roughly one person in five contacted by a Facebook pal acted on the request, mobilizing 5 million Obama-friendly voters.

For fundraising, the campaign developed a solution called Quick Donate, a software program that enabled people to donate money via text, online or email without having to re-enter credit card information: it was designed to be the Amazon One-Click of political fundraising. Those who signed up gave around four times as much as other types of donor. And there was another strategic element: timing. The campaign's marketing team hit prospective donors when they thought they would be most receptive – after a debate, a campaign rally or an announcement by a senior Republican. The figures spoke for themselves: Obama raised $500 million for this first presidential campaign; in 2012 he raised close to $700 million.[6]

Obama's marketing campaign was the most sophisticated that had ever been used in any political campaign up to that time, and it changed political campaigning as we know it. Today every politician with aspirations to public office takes a page or two from Obama's playbook. Obama's online campaigns from 2008 and 2012 were seminal marketing campaigns with relevance beyond the political landscape. They became case studies inspiring marketers across the world to this day.

By embracing Outside Insight, Obama took advantage of social media and all the other information that was available and used technology to connect the dots. His real-time analysis of voter intentions helped his team to allocate its scarce resources in an optimal way. According to one senior official quoted on CNN, they were able to 'run the election 66,000 times every night'.[7] Embracing Outside Insight, Obama understood the voters' shifting sentiments better than anyone and used his insights to become the President of the USA. Twice.

Obama's bid for re-election in 2012 illustrates how marketing has changed in two of the three ways discussed at the beginning of this chapter. It illustrates the new role of technology and analytics, and how powerful social media are in developing a deep and detailed understanding of your target audience.

## *From share of mind to social proof*

Marketing used to be about being as visible as possible, so that when a person thought about your type of product, your brand would come immediately to mind. That is how Kleenex became your tissue paper, Levi's became your jeans and Hoover became your vacuum cleaner. One can argue that the word 'consumers' in itself is a product of this thinking. People and prospective clients were described through the lens of corporate objectives, as recipients of marketing messages converting them to consumers of products and services.

Today marketing has been forced to rethink this approach. Social media have transformed consumers into active researchers, and they have become quite cynical to anything that is promoted directly from companies themselves. Instead, they are looking for social proof. What do other people say about the product? What do people say about competing products?

TripAdvisor is an example of a social media site that has become an online hub where previous customers share their experiences and reviews to help others make informed decisions in the future. Yelp has become the same for restaurants. Positive reviews on TripAdvisor or Yelp can multiply a business's revenue. Negative reviews can push a firm out of business.

We also find the same pattern in business-to-business (B2B). According to the 2014 State of B2B Procurement

Study by the Acquity Group (part of Accenture Interactive), 94 per cent of business buyers do some form of online research before making a purchase decision.[8]

Word of mouth has always been important in creating a company's brand, but since the introduction of social media word of mouth has become king. Your online reputation is invaluable, and the purchase decision of every new client is informed by his or her opportunity to consult the public record created from the aggregate of every client that has ever engaged with you in the past.

Social media are where the bulk of your online reputation is created today. This is the battleground where all existing, lost and prospective customers discuss your strengths and weaknesses. For this reason social media are arguably the most important arena for marketers today. They are also the hardest. It is a new field, barely a decade old, under constant development.

The rest of this chapter will study three companies that have used social media to their advantage in a masterful way. The companies operate in widely different areas of business, but what they have in common is that they have understood the power of social proof and the need to mobilize satisfied customers to vouch for their products. None of the companies has spent much money on traditional marketing, but they have instead chosen to channel their resources into building a community of loyal clients on social media. The result in each case has been a strong online currency and a brand that is loved and trusted by millions. In the process they have also built very successful businesses.

### *The rise of Instagram marketing pioneer Daniel Wellington*

Daniel Wellington is a Swedish watch company that, unlike many watch companies, started with the strap. In 2006 Filip Tysander was backpacking through Australia when he met an intriguing British gentleman wearing a Rolex Submariner on his wrist with a weathered black-and-grey nylon band, known as a NATO strap. His name? Daniel Wellington. Inspired by his chance encounter's impeccable but unpretentious style, Filip decided to create a company for affordable watches with minimalistic, refined designs and interchangeable, colourful nylon straps.

The Daniel Wellington (DW) watch company was started in 2011 and chose early on an unconventional marketing strategy. The founder, Tysander, is famously known for refusing to pay for traditional marketing (although researching him online for this book definitely shows me that he has become big on re-targeting, as his watches have started to follow me from site to site). Instead, he embraced social media and is considered to be one of the pioneers of Instagram marketing. He decided to give away his watch for free to thousands of social media stars. They were given individual discount numbers to share with their followers. Leveraging the fame and credibility of a new generation of social media celebrities, Daniel Wellington entered the watch market with a pace that no watchmaker had done before. In 2014 DW sold more than a million time-pieces.[9] By comparison, industry stalwarts Rolex and Tag Heuer consider it a good year if they can sell a million pieces and have taken 111 and 156 years, respectively, to get to where they are now.

Daniel Wellington understood the new generation of consumers and the importance of social validation. Instead of promoting their watches directly to their target group, they mobilized thousands of opinion-formers to do the work for them.

Scrutiny of the DW Instagram account is revealing. In February 2016 they reached 2 million followers, only nine months after reaching the million mark in May 2015. This is absolutely staggering growth. For comparison, Coca-Cola has only 1.2 million followers on its account.

The most fascinating thing I find with the DW Instagram account is that 95 per cent of the content is user-generated. This is very different from many other brands, which carefully produce content that match their brand story. DW's account is curated, but primarily focuses on sharing photos submitted by fans. To mobilize their followers, DW runs a number of hashtag competitions. By posting a fun photo, or an artistic one, of their DW watch on to their Instagram account, fans get a chance to win an extra strap or a new watch. Some winners are chosen at random. Others are chosen for the originality of their submission.

| | An example of a DW hashtag competition: 'SHARE YOUR BEST #DWELFIE' |
|---|---|
| Step 1 | Take a fun selfie, and make sure that your Daniel Wellington watch is in the photo. |
| Step 2 | Upload it to Instagram and simply tag it with #DWelfie. |
| Step 3 | Tag three friends in your photo and encourage them to post a #DWelfie to improve your chances of winning. (Please note that this is not a necessary step to compete.) |
| Step 4 | Done! |

'Our biggest goal is to maintain an environment that excites past, current and future customers on a daily basis, and to add depth to the brand,' explains Christopher Löfgren, Daniel Wellington's social media manager, in an interview with Kara Lawson of Shareablee.com from June 2015.[10] 'Our followers have a clear and loud voice, and they get to help build our brand, one photo at a time, every single day. One of the best things you can do is to have your actual customers and fans represent you and your brand by giving them a voice and a forum.'

Daniel Wellington ignored conventional marketing and doubled down on social media and social proof. That turned out to be a successful strategy. In 2015, in the fourth year of operation, they posted $207 million in revenue and profits of $100 million.

## Challenging Apple's iPhone with guerrilla marketing and a 'Never Settle' attitude

Carl Pei is an unassuming twenty-six-year-old Swede of Chinese ethnicity. A college dropout from Stockholm School of Economics, Carl has always been passionate about ecommerce. At the age of eighteen he convinced a Chinese manufacturer to produce a custom mp3 player designed and branded by Carl. What he learned in promoting and selling this online would later help him enter the smartphone market and pick a fight with players like Apple, Samsung, HTC and BlackBerry.

In 2012 Carl was working in the marketing department of the Chinese mobile manufacturer Meizu. He was disillusioned by the direction of his company and thought it could be done so much better. A competitor that did impress him was a Chinese company called Oppo, and he decided to reach out to one of their executives, Pete Lau, on Sina Weibo, the Chinese equivalent to Twitter. Carl didn't expect to hear from Pete, a senior executive in a large company with thousands of employees, but to his surprise Pete did respond. Carl told him that he wanted to change the world. He complained that most of the iPhone's smartphone rivals were flawed with bloatware (slow, unnecessary software), cheap plastic cases, unattractive designs and high prices. Pete challenged Carl to come up with a plan for how it could be done better. Carl did, and two years later they founded the company OnePlus.

OnePlus is a smartphone producer based in Shenzhen in China. It offers an Android phone, beautifully designed and with superior technical specifications, at a very aggressive price. OnePlus is able to offer these aggressive low prices partly because they sell their products exclusively online, saving costs on distribution, and partly because they share investors in common with Oppo, the fourth-largest smartphone producer in the world, and can leverage Oppo's economies of scale in procurement.

When OnePlus unveiled their first product, the OnePlus One, in April 2014, with the slogan 'Never Settle', they won glowing reviews. The phone had the best technical specifications in the industry and was being offered at half the cost of a Samsung and a third of the cost of an iPhone.

For its launch OnePlus had a very limited marketing budget and embarked on a controversial marketing strategy to generate maximum awareness and demand. First of all, OnePlus One was an invite-only phone, meaning you could only buy it if you had an invitation. Critics called the system 'maddening' and talked about 'the best smartphone you can't buy'.[11] The invites were distributed through online competitions and referrals from existing OnePlus customers. The invite system created a lot of buzz. The exclusive nature of the invitation made people scour social media for a OnePlus friend or, alternatively, buy the phone second-hand on eBay. Others just became frustrated and bitter because they felt excluded.

OnePlus's first social media campaign was called 'Smash the Past' and received a lot of attention. It was launched on YouTube and depicted a recycling machine where a Samsung smartphone was inserted, destroyed and replaced with a new shiny OnePlus One. People were encouraged to smash their phone on video to prove that they deserve a brand-new OnePlus One: a hundred lucky winners would be awarded with a new OnePlus for the price of $1. Within six days OnePlus received 140,000 submissions. On YouTube you can see people destroying their phones with a sledgehammer, a rotary tool, a potato gun and a freight train. People tried to outdo each other to secure this exclusive phone which otherwise was only available through invites.

During the spring of 2014 OnePlus continued to run campaigns, competitions and giveaways where the prize was an invitation to purchase their phone. For a fledgling China-based start-up launching its début product, One-Plus showed an undeniable flair for getting people's attention. During a twelve-day window where they ran three consecutive giveaways, they attracted more than one million entries, gaining over 40,000 Facebook fans and Twitter followers, over 400,000 unique web visits and 31,000 comments on forums. With hardly any marketing budget, OnePlus relied on its fans to promote its product, and in December 2014, just a year after its launch, the OnePlus website had 25.6 million unique visits.

On 28 November 2014 Carl Pei and his team also showed an impeccable sense of timing. During Black Friday and Cyber Monday, OnePlus temporarily removed the invite-only requirement for purchase and allowed people to buy the phone from the website without any hassle. On Black Friday alone, the OnePlus website received nearly 2.5 million visits – 226 per cent higher than the previous month's daily average. The OnePlus social marketing campaigns had created a pent-up demand that Carl and his team brilliantly harvested during one weekend with an elegantly simple move.

By the time the company neared the launch of its second phone, the OnePlus 2, aka 'The Flagship Killer', customer anticipation had rocketed. When a web page for requesting an invite to buy the new phone was launched, more than a million people registered within seventy-two hours. At a pop-up event in Times Square in New York prior to the phone's launch, 600 people queued up to catch a glimpse of the phone. 'When people queue up for Apple it is to buy the phone. For OnePlus, people queue just to get a chance to see it,' boasted Carl Pei at the time.[12] The OnePlus 2 launched in July 2015, and the number of sign-ups accelerated. By October 2015, sign-ups had grown to 5 million.

The smartphone market is one of the most competitive in the world. BlackBerry, Nokia, Sony, Ericsson and Microsoft have spent billions trying to compete in this space without succeeding. The entry of OnePlus into the smartphone market is like David against Goliath. Unlike the players that had failed before them, OnePlus didn't go head-to-head with the competition, but brought the game to an arena they could dominate. OnePlus had a lot of expertise in social media. They pushed the importance of social validation to a new level, asking prospective customers to crush their old phones. It is an extraordinary example of how a start-up can mobilize its fans to challenge bigger and financially stronger competitors. In 2016, in its third year of business, OnePlus launched OnePlus 3, its fourth phone, which became its fastest-selling device and is expected by analysts to generate close to $1 billion in revenue.

### Shooting for the stars with social currency, PieceKeepers and social diplomacy

On a hungover Sunday back in 2007 three Norwegians in their twenties – Thomas Adams, Henrik Nostrud and Knut Gresvig – just wanted to be as comfy as possible, but couldn't find the right thing to wear. They concluded that the ideal item of leisurewear the day after a good night out would be what you get if you sewed a hoodie to a pair of sweatpants and connected the two with a giant zip. And that's how OnePiece came about.

When OnePiece launched in Norway in September 2009, it became an instant national sensation. The overnight success came as a big surprise to the founders, who didn't even have a logo at the time.

Key to their success was that people took their One-Piece out of their homes and into the public. People wore their OnePiece in the streets, to the supermarket and, in some instances, even to clubs. This trend started when Thomas Adams one day decided to dress up in a purple OnePiece and go out in public to see how people reacted. 'I got so much attention. Everybody asked me "What the hell are you wearing?",' Thomas recalls. 'When people started to ask me where I bought it, I realized that this was something that people would like to wear everywhere.'

The first time I saw somebody wear a OnePiece in public myself, I couldn't help laughing. I thought maybe it was a joke. I wasn't the only one. People's reactions ranged from astonishment to ridicule. The OnePiece jumpsuit has been described as a 'Teletubby' or a onesie for adults. *The Guardian*'s assistant fashion editor Simon Chilvers was not very impressed, according to an article by the paper's Patrick Barkham from 2010. 'It just looks like a hoodie at first but then you get the full reveal . . . it's a bit nappytastic.'[13]

According to co-founder Thomas Adams, the One-Piece brand and products are inspired by 'the art of slacking' or, as it says on their website, the desire 'to capture and conceptualize the essence of a carefree Sunday filled with beautiful nothingness'. OnePiece is unapologetic about their fashion style, and in their brand manifesto they proudly state: 'We're the slackers, the standouts and the fashion misfits.'[14]

OnePiece may embody the 'slacker' lifestyle, but the company is anything but. On the back of their success in Norway they quickly entered the global market and became an international fashion trend. Celebrities such as Lady Gaga, Rihanna, Justin Bieber, the Kardashians, One Direction and Sir Richard Branson have all been seen sporting their OnePiece proudly in public as well as in social media.

'We have never paid anyone to wear our products,' Thomas Adams explains. 'We have not used much money on traditional marketing either. Our focus has been to promote ourselves through social media and through our customers. If we can make our customers promote us, that is much cheaper and much more trustworthy.'

OnePiece has always been a social media innovator. The core of their strategy has been to mobilize their brand advocates (or PieceKeepers, as they are called). Early on they created a way for fans to generate individualized discount codes on the OnePiece website. By sharing those on social media, fans could get kickbacks for all the sales they generated through their friends. The more sales they generated, the bigger the kickback. Kickbacks could be paid out in cash or in OnePiece merchandise. To make a game out of it, OnePiece launched leader boards and 'missions'. By completing missions you could earn points that helped you climb the rankings. Missions were designed to be simple, low-barrier actions such as liking OnePiece on Facebook, sharing a tweet, posting a photo on Instagram or commenting on an article in the *Daily Mail*. By late 2014 OnePiece had grown to a reach of 12.5 million social media followers through their PieceKeeper programme.

In November 2014 OnePiece launched an innovative social media campaign called #SocialCurrency, which received global attention. Every visitor to OnePiece's new pop-up store in New York would get a $1 discount for every 500 followers they had on social media. For sharing a hashtagged image from the store there was another $20 reward.

The campaign went viral, and within a week it reached 21 million people. Justin Bieber re-tweeted a post from Thomas Adams saying, 'Glad we capped our #SocialCurrency discount at $500 or @JustinBieber would've had $312,927 in store credit'.[15] The #SocialCurrency discount earned during the first week was more than $12,000 in total – a small price to pay for an incredibly successful marketing campaign. The campaign had put OnePiece's new store on the map, generated a lot of sales and created international press recognition as a piece of social innovation, but most importantly it had mobilized and strengthened the brand's fan base in terms of size as well as loyalty.

| | The OnePiece #SocialCurrency Campaign |
|---|---|
| Description | Convert your social media following into social currency redeemable in OnePiece's pop-up store in New York City. |
| Step 1 | Visit OnePiece's newly opened New York City pop-up store. |
| Step 2 | Connect your social media accounts to the online ambassador programme called 'PieceKeepers'. |
| Step 3 | The PieceKeeper system calculates your discount based on your followers across Facebook, Twitter, Instagram, LinkedIn, Tumblr, YouTube and Vine. You will receive $1 discount for every 500 followers. |
| Step 4 | Get another $20 discount for sharing a photo of the store on social media with the hashtag #SocialCurrency. |
| Step 5 | Done! |

Another innovative social media campaign launched by OnePiece in 2015 was called #HackThePrice – a tenday campaign where the price dropped 1 cent every time the hashtag was shared on Facebook, Twitter or Instagram (with a cap of 3 shares per participant). At the end of the ten-day period everyone who participated in the campaign would receive an email with a link to buy the slacker wear of choice at the reduced ('hacked') price. On OnePiece's website everyone could track an up-to-the-minute overview of the number of shares and the latest price. There was also a live clock counting down to the end of the campaign.

First time around, the #HackThePrice campaign mobilized 11,000 people to share the hashtag and converted into sales of 7,000 jumpsuits. I asked Thomas how he could explain the extraordinary conversion rate. 'The people that join in on the campaign are interested in buying the product,' he explains and continues: 'Such a campaign also generates a vested interest. If you have contributed to reducing the price, you would also like to reap the reward.'

| | The OnePiece #HackThePrice Campaign |
|---|---|
| Description | Share #HackThePrice to lower the price of a OnePiece lusekofte jumpsuit. For every share the price will be reduced by $0.01 until we reach $57 or the time runs out. Let's do this! |
| Step 1 | Use Facebook, Instagram or Twitter to share #HackThePrice. You can share once on each network. |
| Step 2 | The more people who share, the more the price will drop. Whatever price we hit by 2 June will be the price you can get the jumpsuit for. |
| Step 3 | Done! |

OnePiece's unique expertise is in converting social media conversations into revenue. Through innovative marketing campaigns they have rallied their social followers and generated slackerwear revenue to the tune of more than $100 million over the years.

In order to help other brands to become better at mobilizing their brand advocates, OnePiece has spun out the technical solution offered by their PieceKeeper programme in a newly incorporated company named BrandBassador. Thomas believes that the success OnePiece has developed in social commerce is relevant for many brands and is eager to share what he has learned. 'Every brand has thousands of fans,' he says. 'It is crazy to spend a lot of money marketing to them when they are your own customers. You know who they are and can speak to them directly online without having to pay large sums for it.'

OnePiece has built an unlikely fashion powerhouse based on their understanding of social media brand-building and the importance of social validation in ecommerce. The young Norwegians crafted a go-to-market strategy that relies entirely on their fans for marketing and generation of sales. They have turned social media into gold and have become recognized as innovators in social commerce in the process.

From the initial jumpsuit OnePiece have today expanded to an entire collection of slacker wear, including underwear, trousers, jackets, boots, caps and accessories. Around the world they have ten concept stores and distribute through more than a thousand retailers, and every month they ship to more than a hundred countries. Their objective is to build on the global movement they have created with their characteristic jumpsuit and to carve out a niche for themselves within the global trillion-dollar apparel market. OnePiece has barely scratched the surface of its potential, or, as they put it themselves: 'the slumber party has barely started.'

Daniel Wellington, OnePlus and OnePiece are three examples of a new generation of consumer brands. These are businesses whose main arena of focus is online and which instinctually pay most of their attention to metrics of the Outside Insight type. Their most important metrics are related to social media engagement because they are businesses that rise and fall with the size and vibrancy of their community of loyal clients. These businesses don't spend much on traditional marketing channels because they rely on their clients to spread the word for them. Satisfied clients create the social validation to convince others to jump on the bandwagon. That is the fundamental principle on which they build Outside Insight marketing campaigns. That is the fundamental principle on which they are building a new generation of successful companies.

*Scan the code using the companion app for more case studies and video interviews on this topic. Download at OutsideInsight.com/app.*

*For further reading visit OutsideInsight.com.*

# Chapter Ten

# Outside Insight for Product Development

On 14 July 1995 the noted American cryptography activist Hal Finney posted a crypto challenge online that would later be known as the SSL challenge, short for Secure Socket Layer, a technology that Netscape had invented for encrypted data transfer of information over the open internet. The US banned export of any cryptographic technology with crypto keys stronger than 40 bits, and Hal wanted to expose how easily this could be broken. On 15 August a French doctoral student named Damien Doligez cracked the code using a brute-force approach: he randomly guessed what the key could be more than 500 billion times before stumbling on the right one. It had taken him eight days.

Word of Damien's accomplishment spread rapidly across the internet and was picked up by the major wire services. The media uproar that ensued forced Netscape to come out on 17 August and calm the unrest, stating that it was only a single message that had been cracked – at an estimated cost, in terms of computation power used, of $10,000 – and not the underlying cryptographic algorithm.[1] Netscape argued that their technology was 'strong enough to protect consumer level transactions' because of the cost and time involved to crack a message, but it encouraged people to help lobby the US government to lift their 40-bit crypto key export restriction.

Two months later, on 10 October 1995, Netscape launched a program called Bug Bounty. Probably inspired by the media response to Hal's SSL challenge, Netscape offered anyone that found a bug in its product a financial reward. It was an innovative way to turn an exposed vulnerability into an opportunity. Matt Horner, Netscape's vice-president of marketing, explained at the time: 'By rewarding users for quickly identifying and reporting bugs back to us, this program will encourage an extensive, open review of Netscape Navigator 2.0 and will help us to continue to create products of the highest quality.'[2]

Instead of relying exclusively on their own employees, Netscape turned to the global community of experts and fans to help them make their product better. The awards were not big in terms of financial value, but the acknowledgement of people's contributions was warmly welcomed by the community. Netscape's innovative program – which was later copied by a range of companies, such as Google, Microsoft and Facebook – was built on the insight that, for all its internal brain power, a company can never outsmart the collective intelligence of the rest of the world. Netscape's Bug Bounty program went on to spark a new development within product development, often referred to as 'crowdsourcing'.

Since the announcement of the Bug Bounty program, product development has gone through a radical transformation. The changes have been fuelled by the rapid growth of the internet and the ease with which people can communicate, cooperate and share information across the global population.

Prior to Netscape's Bug Bounty program, product development was a well-defined department responsible for maintaining existing products and dreaming up new ones. Netscape's Bug Bounty transformed their product development into a collaborative effort that broke out of the product development department and beyond Netscape's employees to mobilize a global community of clients, experts, enthusiasts and anyone else that had some time on their hands to chip in.

Product development comes in many shapes and forms. In this chapter we will look at the approach inspired by the Bug Bounty program, through which the crowd is mobilized in order to spur innovations and better products. This type of product development comes in two main formats. It can either be crowd-sourced, where all participants work on the same solution collaboratively to make it better, or a competition can be organized where the best solution wins a prize and bragging rights.

This type of product development is far from new, but in a super-connected world where everyone is just a few keystrokes away there is reason to believe that it will continue to become increasingly mainstream. It is also related to Outside Insight in the sense that it is public, online and fuelled by a global community of participants.

Before we dive into the details of this trend, we will go back in time to get a historical perspective. We will also take a separate look at the open source movement, a movement based on volunteers that took the concept of crowdsourcing and ran with it.

## Mobilizing the crowd: a historical perspective

Mobilizing public expertise to solve a thorny problem is an idea with a long history. In 1714 the British government offered £20,000 for a reliable method of calculating a ship's longitude at sea. It was necessary to solve the longitude problem – how a ship could know how far west or east it had sailed – in order to be able to draw reliable maps and for maritime exploration of the world. It was possibly the most vexing problem of the eighteenth century. Great minds such as Galileo and Sir Isaac Newton had already tried to solve it but failed. The person who won the prize was a self-taught carpenter and clockmaker called John Harrison, who after forty years of working on it solved the problem in 1764. During this time Harrison worked on three different versions of a large sea clock before realizing that the best solution lay with a smaller, more practical sea watch, now known as H4. For many years, however, John Harrison was written off as a fluke. Only in 1772, eight years later, at the age of seventy-nine, did Harrison receive his reward after King George III intervened on his behalf. In the meantime his invention had helped Captain Cook discover Australia. Cook praised Harrison's invention as 'our faithful guide through all the vicissitudes of climates'.[3]

Since the Longitude Prize a number of other competitions and prizes have been announced to spur innovations. The most famous are the Orteig Prize awarded for the first non-stop flight between New York City and Paris, won by Charles Lindbergh, and the Ansari X Prize, a prize awarded for the first successful privately funded space travel.

An area that developed a particular propensity for mobilizing the crowd to come up with innovations was the software industry. Traditionally, prizes were based on the idea of one big prize to solve one big problem. Netscape's Bug Bounty program paved the way for a new approach. In this program everyone was working on the same solution and collectively made it better. This is the approach that became known as crowdsourcing.

The term was coined by *Wired* editors Jeff Howe and Mark Robinson in 2006 to describe the new trend by which companies solicit contributions from the open community to come up with product improvements, ideas, services or data, instead of relying exclusively on their employees and suppliers. Howe and Robinson credited

James Surowiecki's best-selling book from 2004, *The Wisdom of Crowds*, as their inspiration, while Surowiecki in turn acknowledged a debt to Charles Mackay's book *Extraordinary Popular Delusions and the Madness of Crowds*, from 1841.

Crowdsourcing went on to become an incredibly powerful idea that first transformed the world of tech and later became a tremendous influence on innovation, problem-solving and product development across all industries. In my research for this book I regularly consulted Wikipedia, the world's largest encyclopaedia, launched by Jimmy Wales and Larry Sanger in 2001. Wikipedia quickly grew into a global movement of millions of trivia enthusiasts, making it one of the world's central depositories for aggregated knowledge. In the table below, key prizes or crowdsourcing events through history are listed. Some of these will be discussed in more detail later in this chapter.

| | |
|---|---|
| 1714 | The British government offers a 'Longitude Prize' of £20,000 for a reliable method of calculating a ship's longitude. The prize is won by self-taught clockmaker John Harrison. |
| 1884 | First publication of the 'A' fascicle of the *Oxford English Dictionary* (*OED*), which used 800 readers to catalogue words. |
| 1916 | Planter Peanuts holds a contest to develop a logo. A fourteen-year-old boy wins with his submission Mr. Peanut and creates an iconic logo that is recognizable to this day. |
| 1919 | The Orteig Prize of $25,000 is offered in 1919 by French hotelier Raymond Orteig for the first non-stop flight between New York City and Paris. (Won in 1927 by Charles Lindbergh.) |
| 1981 | The publication of the third *Lonely Planet* travel guide ushers in an era of user-contributed updates, tips and corrections from independent travellers. |

| 1983 | Richard Matthew Stallman (often known as rms) starts the GNU project, the starting-point for the movement for free and open-source software. |
| 1991 | Linux is created by Finnish software engineer Linus Torvalds. |
| 1995 | Netscape launches the world's first Bug Bounty program. |
| 1996 | Netflix launches the million-dollar Netflix Prize for anyone who can better their algorithm for film recommendations. |
| 1996 | The Ansari X Prize of $10 million is offered by the XPRIZE foundation for the first successful privately financed space travel. |
| 1999 | The Apache Software Foundation is founded. |
| 2000 | The Millennium Prize Problem is announced by the Clay Mathematics Institute, which offers $1 million to anyone who can solve one of the seven most difficult mathematical problems of our time. |
| 2001 | Online encyclopaedia Wikipedia is launched by Jimmy Wales and Larry Sanger. |
| 2005 | Microtask platform Mechanical Turk is launched by Amazon. |
| 2009 | Crowdfunding site Kickstarter launched. |

Mobilizing the crowd: a historical perspective

## The free software movement

In 1991 the famed Finnish computer scientist Linus Benedict Torvalds, motivated by the idea of a free operating system that anyone could use and change, created what was later named Linux. Over the years he received help from more than ten thousand computer scientists across the world who shared his vision. All volunteering. All contributing for free. Today Linux is the world's most successful operating system. It runs on a third of all the web servers in the world, and Android, which is based on the Linux kernel, runs on more than 50 per cent of all the world's mobile devices.[4]

Linux was part of the free software and open source movement that grew out of the work of Richard Matthew Stallman (often known by his initials, rms) and the GNU project, which he started in 1983. Stallman, although not well known outside of the tech world, is arguably the most influential person in contemporary software development. His work has inspired the creation of thousands of software programs offered for free and with open-source code. In addition to operating systems such as Linux, there are web servers, databases, search engines, programming languages and countless frameworks created with his vision of public-domain software to the benefit of our society. So far, he has received fifteen honorary doctorates from universities around the world for his important contributions. Millions of entrepreneurs, scientists and computer enthusiasts have benefited from Stallman's work. Google, Yahoo, Amazon, Facebook, Twitter and countless other companies are built on software that was inspired by his open-source vision. Research teams all over the world have been able to focus their time undisturbed on advancing their research, building on open-source frameworks for mathematical computation and data visualization created in the spirit of Stallman's work.

I am also indebted to Stallman and the open-source community. When Meltwater was founded in 2001, with only $15,000, we built the company on the famous

LAMP stack, where L stands for the Linux operative system, A is for the free Apache web server, M is for the free MySQL database and P is for Perl, the free open-source programming language. Without open-source software – or without a substantial amount of funding to pay for all the foundational software required – it would be impossible for a small start-up like Meltwater to get started and grow.

Today open-source software is more trusted than commercial software in spite of being created by self-organizing volunteers working for free. The movement started out as an activist movement to protect people's freedom to use, study, distribute and modify software as they pleased. It was a counter-movement to the commercial forces that were driving patents, copyright and other restrictions on intellectual property. Today the open-source movement builds and supports some of the world's most critical and widely used software. From its humble beginnings it has grown to become much more dominant than any of the software giants it originally opposed. It continues to attract some of the world's brightest minds who want to use their talent for the greater good, and as long as this continues to be the case, the open-source movement will continue to produce software that will benefit us all.

## *Crowdsourcing in modern product development*

Modern-day companies have increasingly started to adopt the ideas of crowdsourcing in their product development process. Starbucks received many accolades for their My Starbucks Idea, a site where they ask their fans to come up with ideas for how Starbucks can do better. It was launched in 2008 and positioned the company as one of the early corporate adopters of social media engagement. Within its first five years it received 150,000 suggestions for improvements on products, the in-store experience and corporate social responsibility, and collected more than 2 million votes from customers choosing their favourite ideas.[5] Perhaps the most famous innovation to come out of this program was the famous splash stick, the first idea that Starbucks put into practice. Since then hundreds of ideas have been implemented, including new drinks (Skinny Mocha, Mocha Coconut Frappuccino, Hazelnut Machiatto, Pumpkin Spice Latte), sugar-free syrups, tall reusable cold cup tumblers and free Wi-Fi.

In 2013 the British grocery chain Tesco launched an innovative social campaign to create the 'world's first social wine'. Tesco asked their customers and the internet as a whole to help them choose between five candidate wines (chosen by bloggers and the Tesco wine community), design a bottle and create the name for a new wine to be sold through Tesco's national and international chain of grocery stores. Through an app that was created on Tesco's Facebook page, Tesco received 1,668 entries within three weeks. A housewife from Buckinghamshire, Rebecca Boamah, submitted the winning name idea, Enaleni's Dream, after the name of the black wine community that produced the grapes from which the wine was produced. The wine was a big success from a brand perspective but also in terms of sales. Within its first few weeks of promotion the new wine had sold more than 80,000 bottles.

The Fiat Mio ('My Fiat' in English) was the world's first crowdsourced car. It was unveiled at the São Paulo Auto Show in October 2010, and was a futuristic concept car based on contributions from more than 17,000 people from 160 nationalities over a fifteen-month period.[6] The Fiat Mio was initially designed to be a tiny project expected to involve a limited number of car enthusiasts, but as the number of contributors grew, the project transformed from being a peripheral idea into a central topic among Fiat executives, designers and engineers. A total of twenty-one categories of idea were exhaustively discussed between Fiat's product experts and the 'layman' contributors. Popular themes were: cabin space, fuel efficiency, noise cancelling, on-board biometrics and design. Fiat's experts contributed to the process through sketches, engineering insights and other forms of assistance that helped shape discussions into proposals that were technically feasible as well as practical. However, both Fiat and the crowdsourcing participants were aware that the concept car might not be built as a mass-market vehicle, and might not even be commercialized. Although the car was never produced, it created a lot of value. The concept car was regarded mostly as a map of consumer wishes and helped shape the development of Fiat's next generation of products. Following the launch, one Fiat executive said that the project has changed the way everyone at Fiat works, sending the whole motor industry to the 'psychoanalyst's couch'.

In Chapter 9 I told the marketing story of OnePlus, the Chinese start-up that entered the global smartphone space in 2015, rose to fame and induced feverish Apple-like viral campaigns by allowing its high-end smartphone to be bought through an invitation-only policy. OnePlus is also an example of a brand that uses its community to guide product innovation. After the accolades it received for its first smartphone, OnePlus received mixed feedback for its second phone, the One-Plus 2. For its third phone, the 'OnePlus 3', co-founder Carl Pei launched a programme called Your Ideal Smartphone, where he actively mobilized OnePlus's fans online to inform all key product decisions. His team engaged with the community on a weekly basis, through polls and discussions, to investigate the desirability of features such as water-resistance, near field communication (NFC), a heart rate sensor, expandable storage and design. The contributions guided the OnePlus team through key product decisions such as technical specifications and size of the screen, placement of cameras, battery, choice and placement of fingerprint sensor and the choice of a new innovative technology for charging the battery. 'The new OnePlus 3 specs, design, and features are the results of the contributions of more than 20,000 people from the OnePlus community,' says Carl Pei. And his approach worked. OnePlus 3 was the fastest-selling device the company had ever made. Between August and September 2016 OnePlus sales had to be halted because they were running out of stock.

B2B companies have also benefited from crowdsourcing in product development. In 2006 IBM launched a crowdsourcing event to develop new product ideas. IBM's InnovationJam was overseen by CEO Sam Palmisano, whose objective was to bring some of the innovations he had seen out of the labs and into the world. As he saw it, these innovations weren't going to get out into the market using traditional development methods. 'We opened up our labs, said to the world, "Here are our crown jewels, have a look at them",' said Palmisano, who committed to invest $100 million to develop and bring to market the best ideas from the event.[7] The event drew more than 150,000 participants from 104 countries and 67 different companies over the course of two 72-hour sessions. The initial 72-hour InnovationJam session resulted in 46,000 posts, which were distilled down to 31 promising product ideas. In the second 72-hour session people analysed the viability of each of these ideas with respect to competition and business opportunities. Some ideas held up to the scrutiny and got stronger, while others fell by the wayside.

Ten promising ideas surfaced and entered an accelerated development program sponsored by IBM executive vice-president Nick Donofrio. The most successful of these projects – including the creation of an on-demand system for real-time analysis of traffic flow, infusing intelligence into the world's utility grids, the introduction of smart healthcare payment systems and a new business unit to provide solutions and services that would directly benefit the environment – became part of the IBM Smarter Planet agenda and, according to IBM, have since generated billions of US dollars in revenue for the company.

## Competitions: the prize for innovation

Another well-proven type of crowdsourcing is the financial prize awarded to somebody who comes up with the solution to an important unsolved problem. Such prizes have historically been common in the field of science and mathematics. Earlier we discussed the historic Longitude Prize and the $25,000 Orteig Prize, which was offered in 1919 by French hotelier Raymond Orteig to the first non-stop flight between New York City and Paris. Six people died and several were injured competing for the prize, which was finally won in 1927 by an underdog, Charles Lindbergh, in his aircraft *Spirit of St. Louis*.[8] The prize sparked investment in the aviation space worth many times the value of the prize itself and paved the way for modern commercial aviation.

More recently, monetary prizes have also been used successfully in driving innovation and product development. The allure for participants in many such competitions has been partly money and partly fame.

A prize inspired by the Orteig Prize was the Ansari X Prize of $10 million offered in May 1996 by the XPRIZE foundation to the first privately funded team that could put three people into space twice within two weeks. The prize, created to spur the development of low-cost space flights and the brainchild of the Greek-American entrepreneur Peter H. Diamandis, was originally known as the X Prize, but was later renamed following a multi-million-dollar contribution from tech entrepreneurs Anousheh Ansari and Amir Ansari.[9] More than $100 million was invested in new technologies in pursuit of the prize. The prize was finally won on 4 October 2004 by the aircraft SpaceShipOne, designed by aerospace engineer Burt Rutan and financed by Microsoft co-founder Paul Allen. The prize has since inspired entrepreneurs such as Tesla founder Elon Musk, Amazon founder Jeff Bezos and Virgin founder Richard Branson to launch their own companies seeking to make space travel financially viable and widely attainable.

On 2 October 2006 Netflix, at the time a mail order service for video subscription, announced an X-Prize-inspired competition that became highly publicized and marked the point where scientific awards entered the realm of commercial product development. Netflix offered a prize of $1 million to anyone who could beat their own algorithm for automated film recommendation by at least 10 per cent.[10] The competition was planned to last five years, and on each anniversary of the launch a 'Progress Award' of $50,000 would be given to the best algorithm in the competition to date. Thousands of teams from 186 countries made submissions. Six days into the competition, on 8 October, the first team had already beaten Netflix's algorithm. Thirteen days in, on 15 October, the first team was joined by two more. The results took Netflix by surprise, because their machine-learning team was considered one of the best in the world. 'We thought we built the best darn thing ever,' said CEO Reed Hastings. Geoffrey Hinton, a computer science professor at the University of Toronto, was less surprised. 'In effect, the company has recruited a large fraction of the machine learning community for almost no money,' he said. Three years after the competition was announced, on 21 September 2009, a seven-person team of statisticians, machine-learning experts and computer engineers from the US, Austria, Canada and Israel – a merger of two independent teams – won the $1 million prize and the bragging rights that went with it.

In September 2011 a group of people with no medical training made an important contribution towards a cure for AIDS. An AIDS puzzle that had baffled scientists for fifteen years was solved in ten days by competitors in an online collaborative game called Foldit. For years an international team of scientists had been trying to establish the detailed molecular structure of a protein-cutting enzyme from an AIDS-like virus found in rhesus monkeys. By determining this structure, they would be one step closer to designing a drug to stop the virus. As a last-ditch effort the problem was posted on Foldit, a game created at the University of Washington.[11] Simply put, the game allows players to solve puzzles related to the molecular structures of proteins. No domain knowledge is required, but if a user comes up with a molecular structure with a lower energy state than any of the existing ones, his or her score goes up. 'People have spatial reasoning skills, something computers are not yet good at,' said Seth Cooper, Foldit's lead designer and developer. To everyone's bafflement, a team called The Contenders, with no biochemical background, was able to solve the monkey virus puzzle within days. The winning team comprises members from Canada, the US, Europe and New Zealand, and cooperates through Foldit's built-in chat functionality. A team member known only by the user name Mimi describes how she came up with the solution:

> I had looked at the structure of the options we were presented with and identified that it would be better if the 'flap' could be made to sit closer to the body of the protein, but when I tried this with my solo solution, I couldn't get it to work. However, when I applied the same approach to the evolved solution that had been worked on by other team members, I was able to get it to tuck in, and that proved to be the answer.

Zoran Popović, director of the University of Washington's Center for Game Science, said: 'Foldit shows that a game can turn novices into domain experts capable of producing first-class scientific discoveries.'

Another company applying competitions to create innovations in the medical field is the pharmaceutical giant Merck. In August 2012 Merck launched a competition called the Merck Molecular Activity Challenge, which offered a prize of $40,000 to the team that could create the best algorithm for predicting a molecule's potential to become an effective drug. Participants were given fifteen data sets for biologically relevant targets, each with chemical structure information for thousands of individual molecules. The competition lasted for only sixty days but attracted almost three thousand entries. The winning team was led by George Dahl, a PhD student in computer science from the University of Toronto. In only two months, and without any prior domain knowledge, Dahl and his team were able to develop an algorithm that created a 17 per cent improvement over industry benchmarks. Dahl's team created their breakthrough results by applying recent innovations within a field of data science called deep learning neural networks, methods that had never previously been applied in pharmaceutical research. Crowdsourcing brought new innovations within data science into Merck's R&D department and sparked a lot of enthusiasm for the future potential of novel data science methods in the pharmaceutical industry as a whole.

Mobilizing the crowd in order to spur innovations and new products is an innovative and powerful way to build products. The main advantage of tapping into the broader community for ideas and innovations is that no company, regardless of how large and resourceful it is, will ever be able to out-innovate the rest of the world. In this chapter we have seen how innovation and product development have been spurred by crowdsourcing and prize competitions in industries as varied as Merck and Fiat.

This is a trend that will continue to grow. Indicative of this is the growth of outfits such as Kickstarter, a public benefit corporation and crowdfunding platform that claims to have raised close to $2 billion to help implement creative projects.[12] Its most famous project is probably the Pebble smartwatch. The project famously reached its goal of raising $500,000 in seventeen minutes and a total of more than $20 million to build their first smartwatch.[13] This spearheaded Pebble into smartwatch stardom, but, in spite of having an early lead in the area, it ended up being acquired in December 2016 by its larger competitor, Fitbit.

Another indication of the growing trend towards open collaborative product development is the growth of open APIs (Application Programming Interfaces), which allow software applications to communicate with one another. Most software companies today are launching open APIs. If the client needs a special functionality, they are fully empowered to build such capability themselves. This is an elegant way to 'outsource' part of the product development to clients and partners.

Apple took this strategy and ran with it when they created the App Store for their iPhone. Prior to the App Store, phone manufacturers had usually shipped the phones with their own software. Instead of trying to anticipate all the needs their clients would have, Apple effectively outsourced the product development to their clients. This created a rich choice of apps that made the iPhone very hard to replace. The App Store was probably one of the critical moves in allowing Apple to acquire and maintain its dominance of the high-end smartphone market. A range of companies are following suit. Salesforce's strong app ecosystem is one of its most compelling arguments for anyone wanting to choose a CRM platform.

Crowdsourced product development is here to stay. It is an effective way to make customers actively engage in creating the product they would like to have. No internal product department will ever be able to match that.

*Scan the code using the companion app for more case studies and video interviews on this topic. Download at OutsideInsight.com/app.*

*For further reading visit OutsideInsight.com.*

# Chapter Eleven

# Outside Insight for Risk Management

In 2004 Dr Philippa Darbre sparked widespread concern about parabens, man-made chemicals used as a
preservative in cosmetics, moisturizers, deodorants,
shampoos and tanning products. A paper published by
Darbre in *The Journal of Applied Toxicology*, titled 'Concentrations of Parabens in Human Breast Tumours', suggested
that the chemical could be carcinogenic.[1] Dr Darbre's
research was challenged by a number of large beauty
and cosmetic companies, but in 2005 the EU banned
products above specific concentration levels, based on a
risk assessment carried out by an independent advisory
body, the Scientific Committee on Consumer Products.[2]

A company that approached this issue conscientiously
was Reckitt Benckiser, a multinational consumer goods
organization based in Slough in the UK, with sales in
almost two hundred countries. The company owns a
number of well-known household brands, including
Vanish, Calgon, Nurofen and Finish. Given the complex nature of the ingredients in its products, the
company uses Meltwater to monitor online conversations regarding chemicals and health that could affect
the perception of its brands.

Reckitt Benckiser responded to public concern about

parabens by deciding to reformulate, replace or discontinue the sixty-four products that contained the preservative. The initiative was completed by the end of 2015, by which time the company's chemists and microbiologists had discovered viable alternatives.

This was no mean feat. Websites have been established listing the ingredients in each of the company's products, and external data sources such as social media are monitored in order to predict which ingredients might become future topics of consumer concern. The cost of changing ingredients in mass-produced household cleaning products is significant from R&D all the way through the supply chain to processing plants in multiple territories. Before Reckitt Benckiser makes these changes, the threat to consumers and/or its reputation needs to be properly assessed.

The company established a task force comprising R&D, communications, legal and compliance specialists, sustainability representatives and experts in raw materials in order to use timely, external insights to make predictions for which ingredients might become hot topics and then create initiatives on education around them. The programme, Better Ingredients, was based on external insights mined from publicly available data, and established a governance model for ingredients that enabled the company to be more proactive in its actions.

As part of this, the company established a 'Restricted Substances List', which created a palette of alternative ingredients for the formulators to combine in order to create a product and act as a way for the company to communicate its work in the area.[3] The group met quarterly to examine trends revealed by the external data sources and make recommendations. The initiative was partly future-proofing, partly an exercise in competitive advantage as, by understanding the online conversation around its ingredients, the company was able to make early decisions regarding any action that it might need to take.

The parabens controversy is just one of many issues that can flare up because of consumer concerns about ingredients. A controversy doesn't have to be caused by a chemical that is directly harming consumers; it could be an ingredient that customers view negatively because of its impact on the environment. For instance, there is now an index that identifies companies that are using unsustainable palm oil.

Palm oil is a type of edible vegetable oil that is derived from the fruit grown on the African oil palm tree. Palm oil is estimated to be in around 50 per cent of all packaged items in supermarkets and is a common ingredient in margarine, biscuits, bread, breakfast cereal, instant noodles, shampoo, lipstick, candles, detergents, chocolate and ice cream.

Today, 85 per cent of all palm oil is produced in and exported from Indonesia and Malaysia,[4] but most of the time it is not produced sustainably, causing rapid deforestation, habitat loss and the destruction of communities.

Many believe that palm oil plantations reduce orang-utan populations and threaten other endangered species, such as tigers, rhinoceroses and elephants, indigenous to Malaysia and Indonesia. The World Resources Institute estimates that Indonesia lost more than 6 million hectares of primary forest – an area half the size of England – between 2000 and 2012.[5] For this reason a lot of companies have been forced to consider alternatives to palm oil or to investigate producing palm oil in a more environmentally friendly way. A word cloud created by news and social media coverage in April 2016 of palm oil illustrates key areas of concern.

### Assessing risk in real time

In the high-stakes world of hostage negotiation, one Meltwater client, Hazelwood Street, uses Outside Insight to quantify the risk in any longitude and latitude in the world, any city or state, any municipality, down to regions within cities, in order to help its clients stay out of trouble both in advance and on a real-time basis. 'Nobody in our industry was doing that – they take the cases as they come and off they go,' says Bruce Kaplan, the firm's managing director. Hazelwood Street is a Miami-based company that provides crisis management, prevention and response services, as well as country and political risk management.

The organization is led by the former head of the Defense Intelligence Agency, General Pat Hughes, and its chairman is Cresencio S. Arcos Jr, the former Assistant Secretary of State under George H. W. Bush and then Assistant Secretary of Homeland Security under George W. Bush. The group is responsible for responding to kidnappings for ransom, extortion and terrorism threats across the globe on behalf of two Lloyd's of London syndicates.

'From our experience in the intelligence community we knew that human intelligence and electronic intelligence are the best indicators, so we wanted to develop a more real-time, more robust way of looking at data and measuring it through a proprietary algorithm in order to simplify it,' Kaplan explains.

Kaplan and the team established a scale from 1 to 5 to describe the level of danger of a country. On this scale 1 is an extremely low risk – say, Switzerland – and 5 is a severe risk – for instance, Afghanistan. Once the score is determined, it's then more straightforward for

Hazelwood Street and its clients to evaluate and respond to risk by examining anecdotal data regarding recent events, both in social media and in mainstream news reporting, and to get an idea of metrics such as the threshold for ransom payments, in order to conduct cases accordingly.

'We believe in prevention, and that is really where the data comes in handy,' Kaplan says. 'We are able to give clients factual and anecdotal real-time evidence that there is a problem.'

Every hour data analysts at Hazelwood Street combine data from Meltwater with their own database of multiple other sources – public and private, classified and unclassified. 'Within the intelligence community the realization is that Open Source Intelligence is very, very valuable across the whole spectrum of messaging through news, sentiment and measurement,' Kaplan says. 'Combined with Human Intelligence and Signal Intelligence, it's a really powerful predictive tool.'

Hazelwood Street's software's predictive capability first had a time frame of fifteen days. Then the horizon moved to thirty days, and it is now at six months. Data points include political stability, validity of contract, social justice, the criminal justice system and corruption, as well as low-level crime. A score of 5 means that clients should proceed with caution and allow Hazelwood Street to follow them during their journey.

'Kidnapping truly is a business and we try and keep it on that level,' Kaplan says. Data is employed in every case in order to speed up the process. 'We had a case in February 2015 where they took an entire bus load of shift workers that were coming out of an extraction industry site. There were nineteen hostages.' The company received a phone call from the kidnappers, who identified themselves as part of a cartel. Operatives at Hazelwood Street considered this to be a good thing – the group are known as professionals who will negotiate.

'We started using our data sources, tweets and intercepts of messaging and some news reports and all the other stuff that goes into our algorithms,' Kaplan says.

> We found that the cartel was saying, 'Wait a minute, we got rid of [the kidnapper] years ago because he is a maniac, he is just a local thug.' So with that information in our hands, we changed the paradigm immediately. We told the kidnapper that if he wanted something out of this situation he had better not harm anyone, so he immediately released twelve prisoners. Over the next three days he released everybody. We were able to save lives because we had data on a real-time basis.

## Tracking the health of your key clients

Risk, of course, comes in many guises, and it's not always as high-octane as hostage negotiation. One important task for many companies is to stay on top of their key clients. This is particularly important if a company is very reliant on a few cornerstone clients.

Outside Insight can be very valuable in tracking the health of your clients. Through news and social media, new developments on the client side, such as redundancies, changes of strategy and other important events, can be identified. By analysing job postings, your client's pace of investment can be assessed. For example, a situation where job postings suddenly dry up is a pretty important warning sign. A concerning development could be that your client is being sued. Such developments can be detected through online news, social media or directly through online court documents.

Sometimes the risks to look out for are very industry-specific. The example of parabens above illustrates the risk of ingredients impacting consumer preferences. If the client is in the financial services sector, it may be important to track government regulations, as changes here can have an adverse effect on their competitive situation. Electronics companies are particularly vulnerable to consumer reaction, so getting an early read on, say, a new product launch can be a powerful gauge of future performance.

Using Outside Insight, one can keep tabs on concerning developments with key clients. By listening to external data, early warning signals can be detected, giving more time to react if an unfortunate situation should arise.

## *Supply chain and partners*

Another area where Outside Insight can be used to detect risk is in the supply chain and other partnerships. Once again, vulnerability is possible if your organization is dependent on specific vendors for a substantial part of the supply chain. Tracking of third-party data – import–export data, for instance – can offer significant advantages in terms of ensuring that none of the companies in your supply chain is having an issue that might affect your own production. Estimates suggest that Apple has suppliers in more than twenty-two countries engaged in hundreds of different factories. That's a highly complex ecosystem that's finely balanced. Should there be a glitch – a shortage of the silicate mineral mica, say, which is crucial for the electronics industry as an electrical insulator in equipment – then the entire production process could be jeopardized. Being on top of critical players in your supply chain is therefore important in order to avoid expensive glitches. In this regard Outside Insight can be valuable in many situations by capturing information available on the open internet before it trickles through via the formal channels.

It is also important to keep a close eye on partners. One area that is undergoing increasing scrutiny from shareholders and lawmakers is working conditions, particularly in relation to child labour. Staying with Apple, in 2013 the company published an audit that revealed that, from 2006 to 2013, 349 child labourers had worked in factories in its supply chain.[6] This kind of transparency can help enormously with corporate reputation, but it requires organizations to burrow deep into the supply chain in order to assess their second- and third-tier suppliers.

By way of compensation, Apple forces any of its suppliers discovered to be employing child labourers to fund their schooling and to continue to pay them until they finish their education. Many enterprises, including Walmart, Hanes, Puma, Adidas and Disney, have faced accusations that they have suppliers with poor working conditions. These third-party suppliers are, more often than not, located thousands of miles from corporate headquarters and issue statements regarding their practices that prove not to be true. Outside Insight can be used to track the reputations and practices of these suppliers and identify if workers are being treated anything other than fairly.

Aside from the ethical issues in themselves, these kinds of scandal can have a significant impact on the image of the company. If you were to end up in an unfortunate situation, you would want to know as soon as possible, and this is where Outside Insight can be invaluable.

## *Know your client (KYC)*

In 2012 HSBC and Standard Chartered, the UK's largest banks by market value, agreed to pay US$2.6 billion in fines as part of a settlement with US authorities over money-laundering allegations.[7] Standard Chartered's fine of $667 million and HSBC's fine of $1.9 billion were the largest ever penalties to US authorities by any financial institution for allegedly breaching sanctions policy.

HSBC was alleged to have stripped details from transactions that would have identified Iranian entities, which could have put the bank in breach of US sanctions. The bank was also said to have moved billions of dollars in cash from its affiliate in Mexico to the US, despite concerns raised with HSBC by the authorities that such sums could only involve proceeds from illegal narcotics.

Stuart Gulliver, HSBC's chief executive, said: 'We accept responsibility for our past mistakes. We have said we are profoundly sorry for them, and we do so again. The HSBC of today is a fundamentally different organization from the one that made those mistakes.'[8]

Around the world banks have been fined for not complying with anti-money-laundering regulations. In some instances such violations have been due to dishonest behaviour; in other cases they have been due to failures in the vetting processes for the client in question. To vet a client according to the strict regulations for anti-money-laundering (AML) and Know Your Client (KYC) is a costly and time-consuming job. Outside Insight can be used to automate a lot of the research required for new clients as well as to produce mandatory annual reviews. Analysis of news, social media, corporate accounts and trading information can be used to identify suspicious sources of wealth and find an associate that is a politically exposed person.

## Activist investors

On 6 January 2016 Starboard Value LP, an activist investor, sent a stern third letter to Yahoo's board of directors, stating that 'investors have lost all confidence in the management and the board'.[9] Starboard CEO Jeff Smith argued that the leadership of Yahoo 'continues to destroy value' and called for new executive leadership and a new board which 'can approach the situation with an open mind and a fresh perspective'.

Starboard Value LP is a prominent activist shareholder and hedge fund known for a heavy-handed approach. At Darden, the parent company of Olive Garden restaurants, Jeff Smith won a proxy contest at the company's annual shareholder meeting to replace every member of the board and installed himself as chairman.

In April 2016 Yahoo was forced to agree to give four director seats to Starboard,[10] ending the activist investor's campaign to unseat the entire company board.

Yahoo was later forced to look for an acquirer, and in July 2016 it announced that Verizon would pay $4.8 billion in cash to acquire the former internet behemoth.[11]

Olive Garden and Yahoo are not the only companies to have been targeted by activist investors. Public companies are increasingly pressured by investors who want to set a new agenda or direction for the company. A quick search on Google brings up the following activist investor news:

- 'Seaworld needs fresh board members, activist investor says.'
- 'Valeant replaces CEO and adds activist investor Bill Ackmann to board.'
- 'Activist investor keeps Amazon in hot seat over gender equity, targets Microsoft and Expedia as well.'
- 'Autodesk chooses peace with activist investor.'
- 'Rolls-Royce caves in to pressure and grants activist investor a seat on the board.'
- 'United Airlines facing nasty fight with activist investors.'
- 'Will Macy be able to stave off activist investor?'

In June 2014 the *Financial Times* quoted Leo Strine, the chief justice of Delaware, where most large US companies are registered, as saying that some shareholder meetings have become 'a constant "model UN" where managers are repeatedly distracted by referendums on a variety of topics proposed by investors with trifling stakes'.[12]

Nobody is insulated from the risk of activist investors. Outside Insight can be used, however, to help assess the risk and flag worrying activities as soon as possible. One way to do this is to keep a close tab on discussions in social media and online news. Another way can be to track share trades by known activist investors so that you are warned if they should come knocking on your door.

Risk management is a practice that often focuses mostly on internal processes. Outside Insight is a powerful tool that can also be used to understand risk related to external factors. Crises relating to brand, trouble with key clients or issues with supply chain or other critical partners can all be detected at an early stage with Outside Insight. This gives a company time to prepare and to do what it can to side-step impending difficulties.

*Scan the code using the companion app for more case studies and video interviews on this topic. Download at OutsideInsight.com/app.*

*For further reading visit OutsideInsight.com.*

# Chapter Twelve

# Outside Insight for Investment Decisions

Akkadian Ventures is a specialist venture capital investor based in San Francisco that focuses exclusively on small secondary transactions to create liquidity for founders and early employees of private tech start-ups. Using its proprietary software, it tracks 14,000 companies that fit its investment criteria – more than $20 million in revenue and growing between 75 and 100 per cent per year.

'We want to work on the Ubers of the world before anyone knows they're Uber,' says founder Ben Black. 'If there's an article in the *Wall Street Journal* that says "this company has a $100 million in revenue and is growing 100 per cent a year" it's over for us.'

Black had been working in traditional venture capital for several years when, around 2009, a couple of friends approached him to sell their assets in technology companies because they needed liquidity. Black helped engineer a few transactions in the range of $5 to $10 million when one day a third party called him. He had been working for over a decade as the CTO of a well-known software company that had $30 million in revenue. On paper the CTO was worth $5 million, but he had no money – he was still living in his student apartment with student loan debt. The CTO explained that he wanted to get engaged, and to do this he needed to sell some stock. But only $500,000 worth.

'It's a difficult size,' Black told him. 'It's too big for one rich guy to write a cheque, but it's way too small for an institutional fund.' Black explained that, if the CTO really wanted to go through with the deal, then it would be a lot of work and would probably involve having to ask ten wealthy individuals each to write a $50,000 cheque. To make it interesting for the buyers, Black proposed to offer the shares at 67 per cent of what he thought the fair market value of the stock was. The CTO happily agreed.

It was Black's light-bulb moment. He realized that there was an opportunity in the secondary stock market; the challenge was finding deals, which was difficult and time-consuming. Black recognized that he needed to write software to identify the kinds of companies that he should work on, 'and make me smart and quick about how we approach people'.

Founded in 2010, Akkadian Ventures applies a proprietary, data-driven diligence methodology that enables the firm to understand the development of the hottest Silicon Valley start-ups and to determine which companies to pre-approve for its investment programmes.

Akkadian mines publicly available data using web crawlers to find data points that are highly correlated with the revenue growth of private companies. Examples of such data points are: how much money have you raised? Who has it been raised from? How fast are you raising? How many employees do you have? How many have left the company? What's your churn rate? How many job listings are there on your website? How many Twitter followers do you have? How many LinkedIn connections? How many Facebook friends? 'All of these data are very interesting,' Black says. 'Essentially our universe is any company that got at least one round of funding from the top 150 venture capital firms.'

Akkadian's software is also used to find individual shareholders in target companies. Analysing information from LinkedIn, Akkadian can identify the first fifteen or twenty employees of an interesting start-up. These are the people who will have most stock and will be the most attractive potential clients for Black's investment company. Akkadian's algorithms can also understand when shares will be available for sale. 'There are certain moments that trigger a desire to sell,' Black explains. 'This can be when an executive is replaced or a company is purchased. Analysing news and social media, our software can automatically flag such situations and help us understand the supply of shares in the secondary market.'

Black and Akkadian's innovative approach to venture investment has been very successful. Out of twenty portfolio companies, the firm has had seven companies successfully exit, with five initial public offerings (Splunk, Rocket Fuel, RingCentral, Opower and Convio) and two acquisitions (Ooyala and Medio Systems). In October 2014, it closed its third fund and currently has more than $100 million under management.[1]

## The wisdom of the Motherbrain

Signs that Outside Insight is taking an increasingly large role in venture investments can also be found in Europe. European investment giant EQT announced in May 2016 that they have raised a $632 million venture fund to be deployed in the European market, aided by a secret proprietary software system called the Motherbrain.[2]

The name of their secret weapon is inspired by an intelligent computer system and fictional character, Mother Brain, from the computer game Phantasy Star II, created by Sega in 1989. According to the Phantasy Star II Wiki, the 'Mother Brain' established itself as a benevolent power and 'fulfilled every dream and desire of those it watched over'. This sounds like kids' stuff, had it not been for the seriousness of the people behind it. EQT, founded in 1994, is one of Europe largest investors, with close to $32 billion under management. To head up its new venture initiative they have partnered with some of Europe's most successful tech entrepreneurs, such as Dutchman Kees Koolen, former CEO and founder of Booking.com. From 2012 he advised Uber on its international expansion, but became founding partner of EQT Ventures in late 2015. EQT's CEO, Thomas von Koch, makes it very clear that the ambitions for the new tech venture fund are high. 'Europe today has venture capital funds, but they're tiny,' said von Koch. 'When it comes to B and C rounds, it's for San Francisco to back. It's dangerous for Europe and for the companies. EQT can take a company from $0 to $40 billion within our portfolio. We want to create a powerhouse in venture in Europe.'

EQT's Motherbrain is a company-wide initiative aiding investments across all its funds. The detailed workings of the algorithms have not been shared, but it is known that the tool collects data from at least twenty online sources, such as the start-up database Crunchbase and the online traffic measurement site Comscore, as well as social media such as Facebook and Twitter. Motherbrain reportedly also utilizes data from EQT portfolio company Bureau van Dijk, which tracks the financial data of more than 160 million companies worldwide. The purpose is to find out which companies are getting traction – before anyone else notices.

## Social media as a leading indicator for a stock's future share price

One of the important data types that both Akkadian and Motherbrain rely on when making investment decisions is social media. In a 2010 survey of over 448 investors made by the advisory company Brunswick Group, 43 per cent said that social media had become an important determinant in their investment decisions. Why? If markets had transparent information systems, every investor would receive all the information about the company – reports, disclosures, press releases – instantly. But in the real world this information is only available occasionally; there will only ever be twelve monthly sales reports or four quarterly earnings statements. In contrast, social media can generate real-time external data, information that can predict share price development.

Social media lend themselves to forward-looking analysis. They can be observed at high frequency (daily or even hourly) and, as customers are researching products online, they will come across comments and reviews from consumers just like them and be influenced by what they read. Sales of a vacuum cleaner that has dozens of positive reviews for the power of its suction, or of a toy that parents report their children quickly losing interest in, will rise or fall according to what people are saying.

A paper called 'Does Online Chatter Really Matter? Dynamics of User-Generated Content and Stock Performance', written in 2011 by Seshadri Tirunillai, of the University of Houston, and Gerard J. Tellis, of the University of Southern California in Los Angeles, examined whether social media chatter is related to stock market performance.[3] The authors chose to compare online sentiment to stock market performance because they felt that it was the truest measure of what executives are trying to achieve: shareholder value.

Tirunillai and Tellis chose very specific kinds of social

media – product reviews and product ratings – as they thought these data types would be less noisy than blogs, videos and networking sites. Reviews and ratings reflect a specific intent; accordingly their content is more clear-cut than other more general sources.

Data from fifteen firms was then collected on a daily basis over a four-year period. Six markets were chosen: personal computing (Hewlett-Packard and Dell), mobile phones (Nokia and Motorola), personal digital assistants/ smartphones (RIM and Palm), footwear (Skechers, Timberland and Nike), toys (Mattel, Hasbro and Leap Frog) and data storage (Seagate Technology, Western Digital and SanDisk).

From June 2005 to January 2010 three media platforms with significant reach – Amazon, Epinions.com and Yahoo Shopping – were the subject of daily computational analysis that measured the numerical values of the ratings, the number (or volume) of ratings posted per day and whether they were positive or negative (the valence).

The team found that 'volume of chatter' had the strongest effect of all the metrics in the study, influencing abnormal returns and trading volume. Unsurprisingly, the volume could be directly influenced by offline marketing – increasing the volume of positive chatter and decreasing the negative.

In their paper Tirunillai and Tellis found that social media were a good predictor for future sales, cash flow and stock market performance. The more a product was talked about online, the more its performance on the stock market was affected.

## The robots have arrived

As the amount of data to be interpreted increases in volume and complexity, AI and robots are starting to make their entry. In 2014 the Hong Kong life science venture firm Deep Knowledge Ventures appointed an AI system called VITAL to its board of investors, giving it a vote in every investment decision to be made.

When this was discussed during a panel debate at the opening of Meltwater's co-working space for data science in Shoreditch, London, in August 2016, the Senior Vice-President of Strategy of Winton Capital quipped that in Winton Capital every vote was made by a computer. Winton Capital is one of Europe's largest hedge funds, with $30 billion under management. Winton has an algorithmic approach to investment, and of their 400 employees, 200 are data scientists. Winton's home page outlines their investment philosophy: 'Winton's approach to investment management consists of treating the investment universe as a large body of data within which we can search for patterns and structures that give rise to a degree of predictability.'[4]

According to an article by Stephen Taub in May 2016 in *Institutional Investor's Alpha*, the online journal for the hedge fund industry, David Siegel, an AI expert and co-founder of quantitative hedge fund Two Sigma, predicts that computers will one day become better investors than people.[5] 'The challenge facing the investment world is that the human mind has not become any better than it was a hundred years ago, and it's very hard for someone using traditional methods to juggle all the information of the global economy in their head,' Taub says. 'Eventually, the time will come that no human investment manager will be able to beat the computer.'

Taub's prediction is not about a distant future but is materializing before our very eyes today. According to the 2016 Hedge Fund Rich List created by *Institutional Investor's Alpha*, the top three of the world's highest-earning hedge fund managers are all 'quants': i.e., managers that rely heavily on computer systems in their investments. Of the top eight, only two (!) managers use traditional methods, where the decision-making is driven by human analysis.

| Ranking | Investor | Type | Company | Earnings |
|---|---|---|---|---|
| 1 | Kenneth Griffin | | Citadel | £1.16 billion |
| 2 | James Simons | | Renaissance Technologies | £1.16 billion |
| 3 | Raymond Dalio | | Bridgewater Associates | £958 million |
| 4 | David Tepper | Human | Appaloosa Management | £958 million |
| 5 | Israel Englander | | Millennium Management | £788 million |
| 6 | David Shaw | | D.E. Shaw Group | £514 million |
| 7 | John Overdeck | | Two Sigma Investments | £342 million |
| 8 | David Siegel | | Two Sigma Investments | £342 million |

**Source:** *Institutional Investor's Alpha*

A striking pattern emerges once you read up on the background of the top fund managers in the world. It turns out that among Wall Street's highest paid individuals you find a former maths professor, a former computer science professor, a former maths Olympian and an AI expert with a PhD in computer science from MIT. It turns out that half of the people on the list are maths wizards first and investors second.

## The formula for beating the market

The best-known of the maths wizards on Wall Street is James Simons, a friendly, white-bearded man with an aversion for socks. Simons received a BSc in mathematics from MIT in 1958 and a PhD in mathematics from the University of California, Berkeley, at the age of twenty-three. After graduation he taught mathematics at MIT and Harvard before he joined Princeton's Institute for Defense Analysis, doing contract work for the National Security Agency breaking codes during the Cold War. After a public dispute with the NSA leadership regarding the Vietnam War (Simons argued strongly for withdrawal), he was fired and ended up as head of the maths department at Stony Brook University, New York.

In scientific circles Simons is a living legend famed for the co-creation of the Chern–Simons equation (1974), an important element of one of the most important theories in modern theoretical physics, called String Theory. This strives to combine Einstein's general theory of relativity with quantum mechanics in order to create a unified description of gravity and particle physics and become 'the theory of everything'. For his achievement Simons was awarded the Oswald Veblen Prize of the American Mathematical Society – geometry's highest honour. During a long life Simons has made many other important scientific contributions. At his seventy-fifth birthday four American maths and science luminaries gave lectures about fields of knowledge that he had advanced.

In spite of his academic success, Simons is best-known today for being an investor – in fact, one of the very best. In 1982 he founded Renaissance Technologies, an investment management firm based on the belief that mathematics and statistics could be used to make trading decisions that would beat the market. Renaissance was one of the first algorithmic trading funds and became extraordinarily successful. Its signature fund, Medallion, averaged a 71.8 (!) per cent annual return, before fees, from 1994 through to mid-2014, according to a Bloomberg news article from 16 June 2015.[6] Renaissance Technologies' unusual returns enabled Simons to ask for unusual fees from his investors. Normal hedge fund fees are 2 per cent for capital under management and 20 per cent of profit. Simons's fund charges 5 per cent and 47 per cent respectively. This has not stopped supply of capital. Renaissance Technologies currently has $65 billion under management and is one of the world's largest and most successful hedge funds, making Simons one of the world's wealthiest men. In 2015 alone he made $1.7 billion, and according to Forbes he has a net worth of $16.5 billion (as of August 2016).[7]

Simons's approach was to hire extraordinary scientists with non-financial backgrounds. He hired some of the world's best physicists, astrophysicists, statisticians and computer scientists. About ninety of Renaissance's estimated 300 employees are PhDs. With no prior trading experience, Simons's team of scientists aggregated vast amounts of data and used maths and science to create algorithms that took advantage of hidden patterns to beat the market. Simons's unorthodox approach and extraordinary success went on to transform how stocks and other instruments were traded on Wall Street. Today, more than 70 per cent of all stocks traded on Wall Street are traded by robots.

It is not known what data Renaissance is using for its analyses, but experts attribute Renaissance's results to the breadth of data 'on events peripheral to financial and economic phenomena'. Another clue to Renaissance's secret recipe can be found in the fact that, when Simons stepped down from the daily running of the company in 2009, he appointed two computational linguists, Peter Brown and Robert Mercer, to run the company jointly. Computational linguistics is an interdisciplinary field concerned with the art of making computers understand text. This is an indication that key to Renaissance's secret recipe is its ability to analyse text, and that its information advantage used for trading is created through real-time analytics of large data sets of text. Based on these interpretations, I will make a bold suggestion. Could it be that one of the contributing factors to Renaissance's remarkable results is that they systematically utilized the wealth of information buried in Outside Insight? The open internet is one of the largest data sets of text. It is technically very hard to mine and therefore poorly utilized. Renaissance, with its unique team of world-class scientists, can solve this problem better than anyone else, and by extracting insights that nobody else is able to find they can create an information advantage that might explain their superior returns. This is, of course, purely speculation on my part, but, as we discussed earlier in this chapter, social media were documented by Tirunillai and Tellis in 2010 as good predictors for future sales, cash flow and stock market performance. The more a product was talked about online, the more its performance on the stock market was affected. Surely Renaissance, as one of the most data-savvy firms on Wall Street, was well aware of this fact before it became common knowledge . . .

As we have seen in this chapter, Outside Insight is becoming increasingly important in investment decisions. In the venture capital world Akkadian in the US, Motherboard in Europe and the board-appointed expert system VITAL in Asia show that this is a global trend. It is also likely that Outside Insight plays an important role in the proprietary algorithms that dominate the trading of public stock and financial instruments today.

Professional investors are now sophisticated technology companies, hiring maths wizards and scientists. In contrast, corporate investment decisions are usually far less sophisticated and are lagging significantly behind in terms of both the scope of data analysed and the algorithmic rigour deployed.

By learning from professional investors, corporates can optimize their return on investment (ROI) when investing company resources. Amazon, for example, uses a sophisticated technology to track and optimize user conversion in real time. Netflix uses state-of-the-art machine learning to recommend films based on users' viewing history. By using Outside Insight to create competitive benchmarks, corporates can use the same rigour to create the optimal investment strategy across a wide range of competitive arenas, such as branding, customer satisfaction and product.

In the same way that public trading of stocks and financial instruments has been transformed by algorithmic models, so corporate investment decisions will follow suit. Corporate decision-makers will have at their disposal a sophisticated software that can analyse in real time a variety of scenarios and, based on the objective of the company, choose the optimal investment strategy in real time. In the next chapters we will study the building blocks of this software in more detail and what other things Outside Insight will bring in the future.

## OUTSIDE INSIGHT IN PRACTICE

*Scan the code using the companion app for more case studies and video interviews on this topic. Download at OutsideInsight.com/app.*

*For further reading visit OutsideInsight.com.*

# Part Four

The Future of Outside Insight

## Chapter Thirteen

# The Emergence of a New Software Category

In the first week of December 2011 the Meltwater executive team held a strategy session in Barcelona. We sat in the basement of the W Hotel trying to create a five-year plan for the company. First we tried to create a thesis about where the world was going. We thought that, once we had a common understanding of how our industry was developing, it would be a lot easier to understand how Meltwater could fit into the bigger picture.

The basement was a dark, damp place with no natural light or fresh air, and after two days of intense discussions we stumbled gratefully out into the Spanish sunshine. Our conclusion after some intense debate was that in five years, by the end of 2016, a completely new software category would emerge. As I've described earlier in the book, this software would be to external data what business intelligence (BI) is to internal data. Through powerful data science and natural language processing it would analyse job postings, social media, news, patent filings, court documents, company websites and a whole range of other data types. By joining the dots across a wide range of external sources, it would create powerful intelligence about competition, clients and the overall industry with a level of sophistication that the world had not seen before. We called this emerging software category Outside Insight.

Enthusiastically, we started to dream about how this new software category would transform corporate decision-making. ERP and BI transformed decision-making into a rigorous, data-driven approach based on all the company's operational data. Outside Insight would extend this to all the external factors that influence a company's future development. With the right software the impact of external factors could be measured in real time, bringing Porter's Five Forces to life on dashboards and in real-time alerts.

On the back of this strategy meeting Meltwater put the weight of the whole company behind a five-year plan to create this software. It started with a multi-year rewrite of our entire data platform. Then followed development of the data science required to connect the dots between a wide range of data types. Half a dozen specialist tech companies were acquired to complement Meltwater's in-house expertise. The first version of the product was due to launch in the second quarter of 2017.

Outside Insight software tackles the technical difficulties of embracing the decision paradigm of the same name introduced in Part II of this book. It is conceptually easy to understand that external information can provide valuable forward-looking insights, but it is no small matter to process the vast amount of data available online and distil it down to practical, actionable insights.

The challenge with external data, in addition to its

volume, is that it is much harder to analyse than internal data. Internal data is normally structured and typically consists of numbers. In contrast, external data is unstructured and typically comprises text. Analysing numbers is something computers are very good at, but analysing text is a much harder thing to do with a computer. It doesn't help that online text is found in a myriad of styles and formats. Tweets, job postings, news articles and patent applications are all text documents, but they vary widely in style, grammar and even spelling. Add to that the complexity of aggregating insights in a consistent manner across all the world's languages, and one can start to see how challenging such an analysis is.

| Internal Data | External Data |
|---------------|---------------|
| Structured | Unstructured |
| Clean | Noisy |
| Numbers | Mostly Text |

The nature of external data is very different from internal. To analyse external data a completely different set of technology is required.

As the importance of Outside Insight becomes recognized more widely, there will be a demand for highly specialized software that can take Outside Insight from vision to practical implementation. This is software with sophisticated capabilities in text analytics. This is software that can cut through the clutter of online noise, is able to aggregate insights across different languages and can join the dots across many external data types. In the same way as the need to manage and analyse internal data fuelled the growth of BI and ERP, so the need to manage and analyse external data will catapult the development of Outside Insight into the ubiquitous piece of next-generation software for decision-making.

## History will repeat itself

Studying the development of Oracle, we can see valuable clues about how the Outside Insight software category will evolve. Oracle started out with a database that could collect and store internal data. As the need for more sophisticated functionality evolved, Oracle added workflow, business logic, visualization and analytics to address specific needs in the different company functions.

In order to cater to the growing demand, Oracle went through an aggressive acquisition spree. During the period 2004–16 Oracle carried out more than twenty strategic acquisitions, worth $45 billion.[1]

Oracle's first acquisition was the infamous $10 billion hostile takeover of PeopleSoft, securing Oracle the world's most used talent management software.[2] The next target was the industry-leading CRM company, Siebel, which came with a price-tag of $5.8 billion. Siebel was created by Tom Siebel, a former Oracle employee and Larry Ellison prodigy. PeopleSoft and Siebel were key building blocks in Oracle's future enterprise-wide software offering. Over the years Oracle added supply chain, billing, revenue management, customer support, business intelligence, commerce, point-of-sale (POS) systems and marketing. In July 2016 Oracle announced the acquisition of NetSuite, the world leader in cloud-based accounting software, for $9.3 billion.[3]

| | | | |
|---|---|---|---|
| 2004 | PeopleSoft | $10.3 billion | HR |
| 2005 | Siebel Systems | $5.8 billion | CRM |
| 2005 | Global Logistics Technologies | Undisclosed | Supply chain management |
| 2006 | Portal Software | $220 million | Billing and revenue management |
| 2006 | Stellent | $440 million | Enterprise content management |
| 2006 | MetaSolv Software | $3.3 billion | Operations support systems |
| 2007 | Hyperion | $3.3 billion | Operations support systems |
| 2007 | Agile Software | $495 million | Product life cycle |
| 2008 | BEA Software | $8.5 billion | Middleware |
| 2010 | Sun Microsystems | $7.4 billion | Servers, Java and MySQL |
| 2011 | RightNow | $1.5 billion | CRM |
| 2011 | Endeca | $1 billion | ecommerce, search and customer experience management |
| 2012 | Taleo | $1.9 billion | HR |
| 2012 | Vitrue | $300 million | Social marketing |

| 2012 | Eloqua | $871 million | Marketing automation |
|------|--------|--------------|---------------------|
| 2013 | Acme Packet | $2.1 billion | Network technology for enabling voice and data services over untrusted internet and Wi-Fi |
| 2013 | Tekelec | Undisclosed | Software for managing and monetizing mobile data |
| 2013 | Big Machines | $400 million | Business productivity |
| 2013 | Responsys | $1.5 billion | Digital marketing |
| 2014 | MICROS Systems | $5.3 billion | Point-of-sale systems |
| 2016 | Data Logix | Undisclosed | Consumer data collection |
| 2016 | NetSuite | $9.3 billion | Accounting and finance |

A timeline of Oracle's key acquisitions, 2004–16

Oracle's shopping spree tells an interesting tale of how ERP grew from a central data depository into a fully fledged enterprise offering.

History will repeat itself, and for external data we will see a similar development. The external data depository is a search engine because external data is inherently unstructured. On top of a central external data depository we will see a growing need for workflow, business logic, visualization and analytics – just as we experienced for internal data. As ERP software, Outside Insight will develop into an enterprise-wide offering with custom functionality developed per department.

Sales departments will be equipped with smart algorithms to scour the internet for breadcrumbs identifying new potential clients. This software will provide intelligence on what to pitch, to whom and when. If you don't know the right influencer or decision-maker, the software will also figure out who's best in your network to ask for an introduction.

HR departments will have robots crawling the internet looking for the best new candidates to recruit. These robots will be able to keep a tab on the twenty most suitable hires, for example, and discover breadcrumbs that can give clues about the right time to approach. Triggers such as promotions, expiry of vesting periods, leadership change, reduced investments, anniversaries or redundancies can all help find the right time to nudge external talents to climb on board.

Finance departments will rely on sophisticated software that mines a wealth of online data in order to benchmark performance with key competitors in real time. Analysis will track key competitive dimensions such as product investments, sales and marketing, and customer satisfaction. The analysis will be broken down in granular detail in order to understand development per market, product and demographic.

Traditional ERP and Outside Insight are two complementary software categories that will have to communicate and work closely together. While ERP is internally focused on operational efficiency, Outside Insight is designed to create external awareness. By constantly tracking the flow of external data, smart algorithms will discover patterns and flag emerging threats and opportunities. As ERP solutions have contributed greatly to helping departments stay on top of their operational execution, so Outside Insight will help each department stay on top of changing external factors.

External data is the next frontier. By systematically and rigorously analysing the billions of data points produced on the open internet every day, the guesswork of today can be replaced by fact-based analytics that can identify trends and anticipate future developments. Conquering the wild jungle of external data, companies will become better at understanding their competitive landscape and where their industry is heading.

ERP and BI transformed decision-making into a systematic discipline utilizing operational data. Outside Insight tracks the external factors impacting your business and will become the next-generation software for decision-making support for boards, executives and departmental functions.

*Scan the code using the companion app for more case studies and video interviews on this topic. Download at OutsideInsight.com/app.*

*For further reading visit OutsideInsight.com.*

# Chapter Fourteen

# Hard Problems To Solve

The potential of Outside Insight is enormous, but it is early days, and in order to tap into its full potential a number of hard technical problems need to be solved.

Insights from external data are not easy to reach. They are buried in massive amounts of data. The data in itself is highly unstructured and comes in a plethora of languages. In addition, the data consists of a multitude of data types. To get at deep insights, it is important to join the dots between what is found in online news, patent filings, job postings, court documents and many other data types.

In this chapter we will look at some of these problems and some of the start-ups that are working hard to solve them.

## *Predictive analytics*

One of the unique aspects that Outside Insight brings to the table is its forward-looking quality. When a company accelerates job postings about new sales openings, it is a signal that it is increasing its investment in sales and that competition for clients will increase. To weave all the forward-looking data points found online into a comprehensive prediction is a complex process and requires a careful combination of deep industry knowledge and sophisticated techniques within statistics and machine learning. The holy grail would be to have algorithms that can accurately predict future customer demand, future sales and future cost developments. With the rich data sets available today, such an aspiration is becoming increasingly attainable.

Many organizations are working in this space, but a company that I find particularly interesting is the Ohio start-up Prevedere, founded by Richard Wagner, which we met in Chapter 8. Before launching Prevedere, Wagner worked at a chemical company called Borden Chemical, now called Momentive. In 1998 the company had interests in food, dairy and industrial products, such as wallpaper adhesives and Krazy Glue. He worked on implementing and administering the company's ERP system, based in Dublin, Ohio. Initially it focused on automating transactional activities and then moved into bolting on applications for sales, marketing and finance. Internal data was consolidated in one repository in the hope that business intelligence systems would offer some insights.

'We put all the systems in and we built some great reports on our data,' Wagner says. 'But key decision-makers in the company at director level, and especially the C-suite, they never looked at them. Even if I put those reports out of our BI system right on their desktop for when they came in in the morning, they rarely clicked through them.'

In 2010 Wagner was walking to a meeting with the company CFO. 'I said, "Hey, what I'm noticing is the decision-makers typically don't look at all the data – what are we missing? What can I provide you that would be of use?"'

Wagner's CFO replied that the charts and graphs he was providing executives with were useful, but, 'it's all internal, historical data that we already know we can't do anything about'. The CFO explained that the owners – at the time a large private equity firm – were after external drivers that would examine industries such as energy, oil, gas, automotive, construction and housing, which influenced the company's strategic decision-making. Wagner's bosses, who were responsible for the performance of a global chemical company with a diverse range of products, needed a broad range of indicators, such as which markets to enter, which to exit, fluctuations in the price of raw materials and demand for products and services in multiple marketplaces. Wagner describes the conversation as prompting 'an epiphany'.

Wagner thought about a possible solution and talked with Kevin Smith, the chief economist of the American Chemistry Council, who had written a paper on leading indicators in the chemical industry. Smith had sourced the data for his work in traditional ways, through laborious research and analysis of statistics. Wagner realized that he could build a piece of software that would automate this process, something that would be superior to the 'guesswork', as he puts it, of economists and industry experts, 'a truly fact-based insight on where our demand was going – not just was it going up or down or that we were in this cycle or that cycle, but specifically how much demand would be and what markets there were for every product that we made'.

Working in his free time, Wagner built the system with the help of a developer and implemented it at Borden in 2011, before striking out on his own. Today his company, Prevedere, is successfully helping Fortune 1000 companies from BMW to Yum! Brands predict client demand and future sales more accurately. It has become a leader in the business performance forecasting arena, and in early 2017 it announced a $10 million funding round, bringing its total funding raised to $20 million from Silicon Valley venture capitalists and Microsoft Venture.

In his funding announcement Wagner is quoted as saying: 'Over the past decade, companies have struggled to integrate big data and predictive analytics into their planning and decision-making processes in a meaningful way. Prevedere eliminates traditional barriers to insights – such as access to real-time data, automated leading indicator discovery and intuitive predictive modelling – which is why global enterprises are turning to us to improve their results.'[1]

## *Natural language processing*

A fundamental obstacle to analysing external data is the difficulty a computer has in understanding text. However, a broad research field called natural language processing (NLP) has been working on this problem for as long as we have had computers. A simplified way to explain NLP is as a technology that helps a computer to learn grammar and the underlying meaning of a text. By using NLP a computer automatically determines a piece of writing's sentiment as well as recognizing a company name or a brand. NLP is one of today's hardest problems to solve, and even state-of-the-art algorithms are still far from perfect, but, thanks to tremendous development in processing power and new innovations in machine learning, NLP is a research field that is developing rapidly.

A start-up called Idibon, co-founded by Stanford PhD graduate Rob Munro in October 2014, is one exciting contributor to this field of practical, large-scale NLP. It is designed to be inherently language-agnostic, which means it is independent of any specific language.

According to Munro, on any given day English is currently only 5 per cent of the world's spoken communication. 'English is already a minority language on most digital technologies and will bottom out at something below 10 per cent of digital communications,' he says. There will be no dominant language. Mandarin will account for around 10 to 15 per cent, English and Arabic around 5 per cent and Spanish a little bit less than that. What this means is that there's a very long tail made up of a large variety of languages.

The artificial intelligence underlying Idibon's software makes no prior assumptions about language, interacting with users in order to build up its knowledge base. Today Idibon functions in sixty languages, including Chinese and Japanese, where there are no gaps between words, languages that are written from right to left, such as Arabic and Hebrew, and languages that have their own unique script, such as Korean.

'UNICEF has used us in about a dozen languages in sub-Saharan Africa,' Munro says. NLP enables UNICEF to deal with critical, complex information as quickly as possible. For example, people in countries supported by UNICEF are able to send a text message to the UN for free. The mechanism was initially established so that the intergovernmental organization could conduct surveys, but its purpose has since evolved. UNICEF discovered that it was also getting a high volume of unsolicited messages: for instance, reports that a village was flooded or that a teacher was assaulting students. These types of sensitive and critical messages required a quick response, or needed to be forwarded on to the appropriate organization.

Idibon has also been working with motor industry clients to understand purchasing patterns by examining social media. 'For big ticket items people increasingly go to social media to see what people in their networks have purchased,' Munro says. This enabled Idibon to identify people who had expressed an intention to buy a car with about 90 per cent accuracy.

'With ten out of the fourteen models of cars we looked at we could correlate intention with actual monthly sales in the US,' he says. 'This is going further than sentiment analysis. This is getting ahead of the announced sales figures. This type of predictive application is valuable for understanding how the share price of those companies might change. Or, if you're inside one of these companies, it's valuable [intelligence] because then you know how many cars you should have on the lots. And, if you're a competitor, it's valuable to know which of your competitors has got ahead of you in the current month and why that might be.'

## Data science

Data science is an umbrella term for statistical and mathematical techniques used to analyse large, noisy and complex data sets such as those found on the open internet. We live in a 'big data' era and are drowning in data – internal and external. The nuggets of insights we want to get to can be very valuable but are often very hard to extract. For these reasons data scientist has been called the sexiest job of the twenty-first century. A big part of a data scientist's job is to compensate for noise and data biases. By eliminating these, it is a lot easier to find patterns, which is the first step towards insights. By applying feedback loops, a computer system can 'learn', and the more data and feedback it receives, the better it will become at recognizing patterns. Such learning is often called 'machine learning' or 'artificial intelligence' (AI) and is a core technique used in the aforementioned 'predictive analytics' and 'NLP'.

One of the most fascinating data science companies in the world is Kaggle, which is based in San Francisco and was founded in 2010 by economist Anthony Gold-bloom and technologist Ben Hamner. Kaggle is famous for organizing competitions where data scientists from all over the world compete for prize money and fame. Many of the problems that are solved in Kaggle's competitions are incredibly hard. The Mayo Clinic crowdsourced an algorithm with the help of Kaggle for earlier and more accurate detection of seizures in patients with epilepsy. Microsoft sourced help from Kaggle to organize a competition that improved the gesture recognition in their Kinetic product. Ford developed a crowdsourced algorithm for earlier detection of driver drowsiness with the help of Kaggle.

A competition that I found particularly interesting was launched in November 2012 with a prize of $100,000, which was at the higher end of the amounts generally on offer.[2] The GE Hospital Quest challenge was an attempt to make US hospital visits more efficient. The company estimated that $100 billion was squandered every year through wasteful processes such as delays in procedures being conducted, unnecessary waiting times, bureaucracy and lost or damaged equipment. Crucially, much of this led to delays in discharging patients, which is a significant drain on resources.

The competition called for teams to build a product – effectively, an app – that would enable users to simplify and optimize the customer experience by delivering an improved level of operational efficiency. Each of the contestants decided to focus on a particular pain point in the system – from helping patients understand their post-discharge care plan better to ensuring that porters were in the places where they were needed, according to patient demand.

The winner was an application named Aidin, designed by Russ Graney, Mike Galbo and Janan Rajeevikaran – respectively, a former consultant turned strategic project manager, an energy engineer and a software developer – who had decided to focus on an area that was estimated to cost US hospitals $17.4 billion per year: the re-admissions process. The approach relied heavily on benchmarking. At the time 25 per cent of hospital patients in the US were re-admitted to hospital from post-acute care within thirty days. Aidin made this process more efficient by integrating data from the discharge management process to make recommendations for post-acute care providers, which means that service providers were freed up from administrative work, enabling them to focus more on positive patient outcomes. The app combines multiple strands of external data, such as information from Medicare, and benchmarked numbers, such as how post-acute providers perform, with information about the patient in order to make the best match for ongoing, post-acute care.

The 'internal' data, as it were, comes from patients' hospital notes: insurance information, home address and the type of care they require after being discharged. The external data is pulled from the 25,000 providers, such as rehabilitation facilities, home health agencies and nursing facilities. Rather than having a social worker pore over the documentation and try to find a facility that best matches the needs of the patient and has the capacity to offer treatment, Aidin pulls in external data supplied by the agencies in categories such as the provider's re-admission rate or Medicare ratings that show how often a provider followed best practice or what percentage of patients recorded an improvement in pain management after care. Aidin also has TripAdvisor-style information collected from other patients who have undergone similar treatment in the same locations.

Aidin is a fantastic example of how data science can be used in an extremely powerful way to combine a large range of complex data sets to come up with ingenious new solutions to provide better healthcare, save money and enable people to make more informed decisions about their own lives.

## *Mining social media for 'likes'*

'Tell me what you eat and I will tell you what you are' is a famous quote from the gastronome Anthelme Brillat-Savarin from 1826. A contemporary adaptation of this could be 'Tell me what you like, and I will tell you who you are'. Social media are among the richest types of content in terms of insights, ranging from consumer insights to competitive intelligence. The most fascinating insights from this data are arguably not those that can be found within the data sets themselves but the insights that can be found about the people behind social likes and shares. It turns out that by analysing a person's 'likes' and shares on social media, information about that person's gender, age, education level, salary bracket, taste in music, political leanings and sexual preference can be estimated with surprising accuracy.

One of the pioneers in this space is Philometrics, a company founded by Alex Spectre, a psychology professor at the University of Cambridge. Spectre uses machine learning to mine social media in order to create rich profiles of the people who actively engage on Facebook, Twitter and Instagram. The initial area where he applies these social profiles is in improving customer surveys.

Today quantitative surveys will ask the customer's gender, age and location, and then maybe ask ten questions about the product they're researching. Spectre's method is to take this information and add social signals to create a much richer profile of the respondents. Think about your Facebook profile – the kinds of things that you're posting and 'liking', the groups that you're following. It's possible to build a very accurate picture of who you are: for instance, Philometrics can make a good guess at your salary and education level.

'The flaw with focus groups that have been recruited is that they are in no way representative of the human race – and that's a problem,' Spectre says. Traditional research methods involve asking a direct question: for instance, which of these two paintings do you like – the Da Vinci or the Picasso? Which phone do you prefer – the one with the touchscreen or the one with the keyboard? 'It doesn't scale and it's extremely expensive to do anything with larger samples,' Spectre says. 'So typically organizations would run a few hundred people and then generalize.'

The other great flaw in the system is the variability in the population. 'You and I are not the same,' Spectre says, 'and lo and behold! Most things that are interesting are not going to be the same. There will be a lot of differences: geographic, across age groups, across income, across gender, across ethnicity, income, political and every which way you want to imagine there are differences. And we usually miss that; we just don't have the resolution to go out and do it.'

The Philometrics insight was that we can leverage social media and other behavioural data sources to scale consumer surveys.

The vision for Philometrics is a platform where organizations can very easily conduct surveys through an automated process that uses machine learning models capable of predicting responses. Clients will survey, say, 500 to 1,000 people, but Philometrics will send back a data set that has, say, 130,000 people. 'Our next step is going to be: how do we make analysis really easy? So you have the 130,000 people, then you just click on a graphic of a map of the US,' Spectre says. 'It becomes a technique that's not just reserved for people with expertise and access to large amounts of data; now it's open to everybody.'

Spectre warns of the limited accuracy for individuals. But he argues that the models are still valuable, because we rarely care about specific people – rather, much market research is predicated on understanding groups of people (e.g., millennial women in California). The methodology Spectre developed takes individual predictions across these sorts of segments. When aggregated, much of the noise in the estimates gets cancelled out, and we get a relatively good estimate of the group average. And these groups are precisely what marketers want to know about.

### Joining the dots

One of the big promises of Outside Insight is its ability to connect the dots between different data types. Imagine if every document published online could be analysed with newly found insights stored and categorized based on their internal relationships. It's challenging for a machine to extrapolate meaning from text that comes from different sources and often in different languages, but knowledge graphs can help to bring hidden connections to light.

For example, analysing patent filings we can find that a person called 'Catherine Larsen' has been awarded a patent on behalf of IBM. On Twitter we see that she loves Italian wine and travels often to Rome. On LinkedIn we can learn that next month she has been with IBM for eight years and that after graduating with a Master's degree in electrical engineering from UC Berkeley in 2001 she started her career as a software developer with HP and stayed there for eight years before moving to IBM.

Mining a wide range of data types we can combine insights found in a graph. Such a graph can be used to find relationships that are not explicitly expressed in any of the data we mine. For example, we can discover that our VP of Engineering studied together with Catherine at Berkeley, that one of our job applicants used to work for Catherine during the year she applied for the IBM patent and that our VP of Sales was in Rome at the same time as her last year.

A graph is a powerful tool for deriving higher-level insights, and an area of technology dominated by frenzied R&D activity at the moment. The fundamental challenges are related to the disambiguation of company names and people. To understand that the inventor of a patent is the same as or different from the person tweeting she had just arrived in Rome is not an easy problem. One issue is that the spelling of her name can be inconsistent. In the patent her name may be spelled 'Catherine Larsen', and on Twitter she is spelled 'Cat Larsen'. It doesn't make it any easier that there can be hundreds of people with that name. People are also frequently changing names. Cat may have married after her patent filing and taken her husband's family name.

An interesting company in the graph space is San Francisco-based Spiderbook. Co-founders Aman Naimat and Alan Fletcher spent several years running internal sales and marketing applications at Oracle. The pair came to the realization that most salespeople didn't use the apps because the software didn't reveal anything about the most important element of their work: the world beyond the company walls.

'Traditional applications are inward-facing,' Naimat says. 'But what do sales people do? Ninety per cent of the time they spent outside the application. Yet, Salesforce, Oracle and SAP are building applications for the ten per cent of the time sales people are spending within the company. So what happens to the other 90 per cent? Technologists were just ignoring it.' What's really useful, of course, is customer intention: will a customer renew a contract? Will they buy the next product? What are they interested in? 'Even if you have a 10 per cent understanding of what a customer is doing in the out-side world you have more information than everything you can garner from the inside,' Naimat says.

Naimat and Fletcher decided to build the next gener-ation of applications based on research they did at Stanford by focusing on the behaviour of a salesperson. Their start-up, Spiderbook, is a knowledge graph that's been built around every business on the internet, with data points including customers, partners, suppliers, the elements that individual enterprises are investing in, the positions they're hiring for and their business priorities.

'In essence, this is the internet, but we throw out everything that is not mentioned in a business concept, like a company, or a product, or a person associated with the business,' Naimat says.

Five years ago, such an endeavour would require per-haps $100 million for infrastructure in order to process 300 to 400 terabytes of data. The cost today is a fraction of that. 'We've optimized the process and machinery so much that we can read the entire business internet and process it at any given time for $750,' Naimat says.

The algorithm, which has been programmed to understand business vocabulary, scrapes data from across the web. Natural language processing means that it's able to discern how people express relationships between, say, a pharmaceutical company and an energy company, or a technology company and a motor manufacturer.

'If you compare our engine to an average salesperson

it performs with ten times more precision,' Naimat says. 'We typically find salespeople's response rates are around 3 per cent. Today we have some clients who get as high as 20 to 30 per cent response rates. The fact that we can read everything is just so much more powerful,' says Naimat.

Search engines before Google looked at key words. Google decided to join the dots and built PageRank, a ranking of linked websites. Naimat claims that the real innovation of Spiderbook is its ability to connect all the pieces, joining together every relevant online data point.

Naimat gives an example of a health start-up that Spiderbook is working with. After searching the web and analysing the millions of companies that it might sell to, the algorithm identified 787 companies that were worth pursuing. 'Not only will it sort of tell you go sell into these companies; it also guides you through the process,' Naimat says. 'Spiderbook is beyond a tool at this point because you're not telling it what you want it to do – it's telling you that you should go sell to Monsanto, for instance, and let me guide you through the process by identifying the individuals who will be most receptive because, say, they're blogging or are sharing a presentation on Slideshare on a particular subject.'

All these new technologies, from Spiderbook's knowledge graph to Philometrics' interpretation of social signals, Idibon's NLP and Prevedere's predictive analytics, are attacking some of the hardest problems of data analytics today. They are not alone. Across the world there are literally thousands of companies that are working hard to solve these problems in myriad ways. Thanks to tremendous developments in cloud-based computing power and constant innovations in machine learning, the prospect of tapping into the full potential of Outside Insight is closer than ever. There is therefore reason to be optimistic that most of the technical obstacles should be resolved in the near future. There is reason to believe that within a few years Outside Insight will be a commonplace aid to informed and timely decision-making in every department and at every level within a company.

# Chapter Fifteen

# New Data Sources

Back in the mid-1990s, when I was a young research scientist in machine vision and artificial intelligence at the Norwegian Computing Center, one of my tasks was to analyse satellite images of the Norwegian mountains. The objective was to estimate the amount of snow in the mountains during winter. This was done in order to understand the risk of flooding during the spring. The data also had another interesting use, as there was a correlation between the amount of snow in the winter and the amount of water feeding Norway's 278 hydropower plants, and therefore also the future production volume and cost of electricity.

The number of satellites orbiting the earth has undergone an enormous rise over the past decades. Over the past few years there has been a multiple order of magnitude drop in the price of satellites and a commensurate increase in the availability of the imagery they produce. In the past those images were just available to governments, but now pricing has come down to make satellite imagery accessible for a number of commercial uses. As pricing drops further, I believe aerial imagery from satellites and drones will be a new and commonplace data source for next-generation business analytics.

## *Orbital Insight*

One company that has taken satellite imagery to the next level is Palo Alto-based Orbital Insight. Using advanced image-processing, machine vision and cloud-based computational power, they use satellite images to determine a wide range of interesting commercial insights, such as estimating retail sales by counting cars in shopping centre car parks, creating independent data about the health of the Chinese economy by measuring the amount of commercial construction work, predicting the yield of crop harvests by tracking agricultural fields and many others.

According to founder and CEO James Crawford, we already have the ability to take 8 million square kilometres of imagery across the world every day, and that will increase by a factor of ten in the near future because of the number of private satellite start-ups entering the market-place, and by another factor of ten as drones become commonplace in our skies and provide better-quality images than satellites.

The new entrants are building satellites that are incredibly small and cost a fraction of what they used to. The growing array of satellites and drones will mean that eventually we will have access to images of every city in the world at every moment in time – a volume of data that it will be impossible for human beings to process. Consequently, analysis will be done by machines.

Deep learning and AI will scale up our ability to look at images and will be able to spot geo-economic trends across the world.

Big box retailers, which have large parking areas, are rich potential sources for accumulating powerful consumer data that can be used for multiple forms of extrapolation. For instance, Orbital Insight can offer its financial services clients predictive data about the quarterly performance of Walmart or other big box retailers by looking at images of car parks. Aggregating several years' worth of this data can produce a heat map that shows where shoppers prefer to park, and other trends such as seasonal patterns of behaviour and other time frames, like days of the week. It's possible to do comparisons to judge which of two competitors is performing better – data that's extremely valuable to investors. According to Crawford, activity in the car park is directly related to that company's stock price.

Aggregating a large amount of data enables us to see macroeconomic trends that offer us insight into the performance of the wider economy with a high degree of accuracy because of the scale of the information. Orbital Insight aggregates data from fifty retail chains across the US in order to get a macro view of the US economy. Commercial drones will increasingly be used for this purpose as well.

As we move forward, Crawford believes that, as well as using this kind of data for financial forecasting, we will understand and contextualize store performance by understanding general trends, understanding customer behaviour such as whether consumers are having trouble getting to a store, the influence store locations have on sales, traffic patterns within cities and regions, and anticipating supply chain disruptions such as bottlenecks in ports or transport problems with major suppliers. Understanding the world as a geo-spatial problem – whether this is images from drones, mobile phone counts or car counts from connected vehicles – that can be analysed at scale can provide crucial data to industries including retail, energy, insurance, health and finance, not to mention government applications.

## Planet Labs

One start-up that is pushing down the price of commercial application of satellite imagery is Planet Labs, based in San Francisco. The company, which has just over $151 million in venture funding, is an aerospace business that uses off-the-shelf materials to develop and build low-cost imaging satellites, known as Doves, that are little more than the size of a brick, with a weight of about 9 lb. These satellites are sent into orbit as passengers on other missions, attached to rockets, and are for this reason much more cost-efficient to deploy. Each Dove satellite continuously scans the earth, sending data once it passes over a ground station. Together Dove satellites form a constellation that provides a complete image of the earth at 3–5m optical resolution. The images gathered by the Dove satellites provide up-to-date information relevant to climate monitoring, crop yield prediction, urban planning and disaster response.

Planet Labs has a very different model from that of a government organization like NASA. Although not directly comparable, NASA's Landsat 8, which was launched in February 2013, cost $855 million to develop and is the size of a truck.[1]

Since its start in 2010, Planet Labs has designed, engineered and launched seventy satellites into space, more than any other company. Once it has 150 in orbit (expected to happen in 2017), Planet Labs claims that it will be able to send back images twice a day that take in the whole of the earth. This avalanche of imagery will create an unprecedented database of the entire planet, one that can be used to stop forest fires and maybe even wars.

### Terra Bella

There are a number of other organizations mapping the earth from space, including Terra Bella, which is a subsidiary of Google. Its satellites are around the size of a mini-fridge – like Planet Labs' satellites, they're built with off-the-shelf components – and send static images and HD video back to earth, where they can be used to understand the movement of trucks transporting products from, say, a distribution centre to a retailer, the amount of wattage coming from a developing nation where uptake of electricity is spreading or the amount of a discolouring pollutant in the bay near a city.

All of this data has governmental and private applications and is as relevant to scientists and environmental campaigners, say, as it is to economists and analysts at financial institutions building forecasting models. If you can examine oil storage tanks from above, you might have a sense of how much is being pumped and added to the world market. If you can analyse the number of trucks coming out of Foxconn's manufacturing facility in Shenzhen, you would have an idea of when the next iPhone is going to be released.

### From the macro to the micro

In July 2016 the Japanese tech investor SoftBank announced a $32 billion acquisition of the British chip producer ARM.[2] The bid was a staggering 43 per cent higher than the last closing price and 41 per cent (!) higher than its all-time high.

The acquisition represented SoftBank's belief in the future of the Internet of Things (IoT) and was an investment in a future transformational technology trend estimated by a 2016 World Economic Forum report to create a value of $19 trillion over the next decade in cost savings and increased profits.

It is hard to grasp such immense value creation, but whether the report from the World Economic Forum is accurate or not, it is pretty clear that the IoT will impact the world in a very big way.

The Internet of Things can be described very simply as a large volume of interconnected sensors with processing powers. These sensors can be embedded in almost anything, almost anywhere. Imagine a light bulb equipped with a sensor that can detect that the bulb is broken and send this information to a janitor who knows where to find a new bulb and what equipment is needed to replace it. Such sensors can be utilized in manufacturing to create efficiency and automation in factories; they can add much more precise data to logistical processes and create a lot of value for processes and businesses we currently cannot imagine.

The interesting aspect of the IoT with respect to Outside Insight is the new data it collects. Admittedly a lot of the IoT data will be company internal data, where it can improve a lot of operational decisions and processes, but there will also be a range of publicly available IoT data that companies can tap into. This is illustrated by some of the smart city initiatives deployed on an experimental level in cities such as Amsterdam, Barcelona, Stockholm and Singapore. As part of these cities' ambition to create efficiency and improve their citizens' quality of life, interconnected smart sensors are deployed widely to identify traffic congestion, optimize power consumption and improve public safety. In the process, a lot of information is collected and aggregated. It is unclear how much of this information will be publicly available, but as sensor technology and processing power become cheaper, one can easily imagine a future where every street, every house, every traffic light and every road junction is littered with sensors collecting data that can be used for analytics.

Satellites and drones are swarming the sky, and on the ground tiny sensors are swarming our homes, our bodies (in the form of wearable tech), our vehicles and our surroundings. When combined, they provide data about imagery, temperature, humidity, pollution level and a whole range of other detailed information.

From an Outside Insight perspective, the Internet of Things will in the future provide a new rich data source that companies will be able to use to predict customer behaviour, future demands, the success of their competitors and a whole range of other insights that today are hard to imagine fully.

The wealth of information available on the internet today is mind-boggling. And with every day that passes it continues to grow exponentially. And that is before the Internet of Things really takes off. As new sensor technologies become more prolific, virtually anything will be measured and logged. The Internet of Things alone will probably produce as much information as all the information published on the internet. And as drones and satellite imaging develop further, virtually every spot on the globe will be monitored and recorded in video, sound, and infra-red.

We have a lot of data today, but it will be dwarfed by the data we will have going forward. The data will continue to grow exponentially. With the growth of the data, more insights can be retrieved. They will increase the potential value of Outside Insight, as long as we develop technologies that enable us to analyse the vast data sets we will be dealing with.

# Chapter Sixteen

# The Potential Concerns of Outside Insight

In November 2016 Donald Trump unexpectedly won the US presidential election. The result was contrary to the traditional polls, which all had Hillary Clinton as a strong favourite. Nate Silver, the journalist and statistician who famously correctly predicted the outcome of every single state in the 2012 US presidential election, was also completely off the mark, giving Clinton a 71 per cent chance of winning on the eve of the election.[1] How surprising the outcome was can be illustrated by *The New York Times* estimate early on the election night that the probability of Hillary Clinton winning was 80 per cent.[2] That figure changed radically throughout the night as the results came in.

**Chance of Winning the Presidency - 8 November 2016**

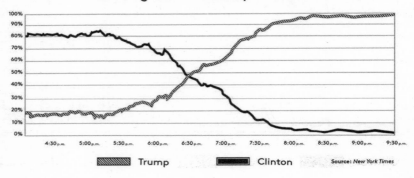

Source: *New York Times*

A few analytics companies were not surprised by the result. An Indian start-up called Genic.ai, which had correctly predicted the winner of the previous three elections, announced ahead of the results that according to their models Trump was favourite to win.[3] Genic.ai uses 20 million data points from online platforms such as Google, YouTube and Twitter to come up with its predictions using artificial intelligence. Meltwater's analysis of social media also showed that Trump had very strong support online, and particularly in social media. The day before the election, we published an analysis of the hashtags used by the two candidates, which showed that Trump was twice as likely to win as Clinton.[4] Similar analysis had been used a few months earlier to predict the outcome of the UK Brexit referendum correctly.[5]

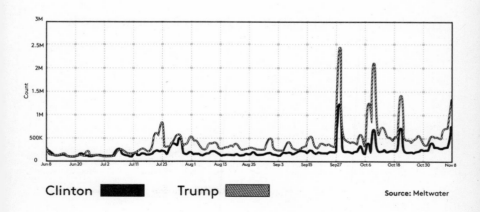

Clinton ▬▬▬▬    Trump ▨▨▨▨    Source: Meltwater

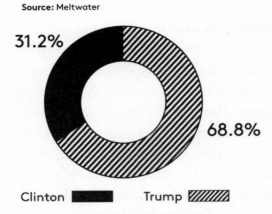

**Source:** Meltwater

31.2%

68.8%

Clinton �  Trump ▨▨▨▨

The day before the election, Meltwater announced an analysis that showed Trump had twice as much support on social media as Clinton, predicting an upset win for Trump.

The conclusion from both the Brexit referendum and the Trump victory was that traditional polls are not as reliable as they used to be and that in these two cases social media had provided better clues to people's real sentiments.

Once Trump's victory was a fact, journalists and analysts tried to understand why the polls had been so unreliable. Although polls always have a certain percentage margin of error, they had never before been so dramatically proven false. What was different in 2016?

## Tell me what you like and I will tell you who you are

The answer to this is not fully understood, but it is clear that Trump's camp doubled down on social media campaigning. Part of Trump's online strategy was allegedly a company called Cambridge Analytica, the US arm of a British behavioural research and strategic communications company called SCL Group Ltd. According to an article in the *Wall Street Journal* on 9 November 2016, Cambridge Analytica is partly funded by Robert Mercer, a computer scientist and co-chief executive of the quantitative hedge fund Renaissance Technologies.[6]

A January article on Motherboard, headlined 'The Data That Turned the World Upside Down', detailed how Cambridge Analytica have created sophisticated psychometric models based on social media activity, which were used to identify undecided voters in critical swing states and suggest how to influence them.[7]

The model used by Cambridge Analytica shows parallels to research from Cambridge University by two PhD students, Michal Kosinski and David Stillwell, who combined Facebook 'likes' with a psychometric model developed in the 1980s called OCEAN, which could be used to predict a person's needs, fears and behavioural patterns. This model had historically been hard to use in practice because of the large amount of survey data it required, but Kosinski and Stillwell used

Facebook data to compensate for this. Their research showed that this approach was remarkably reliable. Kosinski and Stillwell claim that, on the basis of an average of sixty-eight Facebook 'likes' by a user, they were able to predict skin colour (with 95 per cent accuracy), sexual orientation (88 per cent accuracy) and favourable inclination to the Democratic or Republican party (85 per cent). In addition, they were also able to determine intelligence, religious affiliation and use of alcohol, cigarettes and drugs. From the data it was even possible to deduce whether someone's parents were divorced.

Exactly what role psychometrics played in Trump's surprise victory is unclear. Sources argue that using social media data for psychometric modelling is still very much an unproven science. They challenge the importance of this data in the Trump campaign. After all, in the primaries Cambridge Analytica was used by Ted Cruz, who was crushed by Trump, who himself was aided by nothing more than a Twitter account and a simple, static website that he paid a freelancer $1,500 to put together.

### Three areas of potential concern raised by the 2016 presidential election

Regardless of how important the use of Facebook 'likes' was in determining the outcome of the 2016 US presidential election, that election brought to the surface three important areas of concern that are also broadly relevant for Outside Insight.

The first one is that of privacy. As we all leave behind us a constant trail of 'likes', tweets, check-ins and photos, how can we protect this data from sophisticated algorithms that psychometrically profile us and take advantage of us?

The second is the danger of the algorithms themselves. Can algorithms become too smart? Is there an ethical line that algorithms can cross?

The third area is that of fake news. During the 2016 presidential election a whirlwind of fake news was created. Examples of fake news that were widely shared online are reports of Hillary Clinton running a child sex ring out of a pizza shop,[8] of Democrats wanting to impose Islamic law in Florida and of Trump supporters in a Manhattan rally chanting, 'We hate Muslims, we hate blacks, we want our great country back.'[9] Interestingly, such fake news galvanized the beliefs of existing voter bases and eroded the credibility of traditional news sources.

## How do we protect people's privacy?

Many people argue that we just have to forget about privacy in this day and age. With the growth of social media we have opened the door to an era of radical transparency, and many people, such as Google's Eric Schmidt, argue that we just have to accept that privacy is a thing of the past.[10]

Many people don't worry much about privacy because they are oblivious to the amount of information they're sharing about themselves. For instance, if you're out having dinner at a restaurant, you may find yourself tagged in someone else's status update. Or someone may take a photo of you without your knowledge. Status updates and photos are both frequently geotagged, revealing information about your location.

Social media are littered with information about you, such as where you eat, who you socialize with, where you shop, what products you're purchasing and a host of other details of your life. Even if you are not very active on social media yourself, Facebook, Twitter, Instagram, Pinterest and Snapchat will know a lot about you because your friends have tagged you in their social posts.

For many people this isn't something to lose sleep over; they argue that they have nothing to hide. But analysing all the online digital breadcrumbs we leave behind, we are revealing more information about ourselves than we may realize. By analysing a person's Facebook 'likes' or Twitter timeline it's possible to determine with a high degree of accuracy a person's salary range, education level, sexuality and political leanings. Over time, as an increasing amount of data is collected on social platforms and smart algorithms become smarter, profiling will become more accurate and there-fore more invasive.

During a job interview a potential employer in the US is not allowed to ask questions relating to a candidate's age, religious beliefs, sexual preference or political affili-ation. This law is created in order to prevent people from being discriminated against. But employers can now glean most of this information from social media anyway.

The 2016 presidential election in the US and the psy-chometric campaigns by Cambridge Analytica brought to the surface the importance of privacy. As analytics grow in sophistication, privacy is clearly going to become an increasingly important issue.

## When are algorithms too clever for their own good?

When it comes to algorithms, we are constantly push-ing for greater sophistication and accuracy. On the surface it does seem that the better algorithms we get, the better off we are. An example of this is our analysis of customers' social media chatter. The more accurately the algorithms understand the true sentiment of our clients, the better. But is this always the case, or are there situations where algorithms raise important eth-ical questions?

The US retailer Target's data science program made headline news when it was reported by *Forbes* magazine in 2012 that Target had sent coupons for baby clothes to a high-school girl based on her purchase history, correctly predicting that she was pregnant before she had told her parents.[11] Some doubts about the truth of this story have since been raised, but the story still illustrates that algorithms can potentially cross an ethical line.

When it comes to deducing personal or intimate information about a person, algorithms are entering an ethically sensitive area. Skin colour, sexual orientation, political leaning, education, salary level, intelligence and religious affiliation are all examples of information that people don't usually share directly but which algorithms can deduce from a lot of data points that in themselves may seem innocent. This can create many difficult ethical situations. In many countries, such as the US, it is illegal to discriminate against a job applicant on grounds of age, religion or sexual orientation. In some countries homosexuality is against the law. The existence of algorithms that can infer sensitive information about people can in these situations be used for discrimination or, in the worst case, prosecution.

Perhaps one of the most ethically sensitive areas for algorithms is when they are used to profile people and these profiles are used to actively develop strategies to manipulate their behaviours. If algorithms are so sophisticated that they understand which buttons to push in order to provoke a desired reaction, they are becoming dangerous psychological weapons. Many believe that Donald Trump was able to reduce the black vote on the eve of the election when his campaign targeted black voters through social media with videos of Hillary Clinton talking about 'super-predators'. Clinton was accused of using the term to characterize young African-Americans. Black voters would generally be expected to vote more for Clinton than Trump, so the more black voters stayed at home rather than going out to vote, the better it was for Trump.

Manipulating people to vote a particular way sounds bad, but if we think about it, we are surrounded by messages trying to convince us one way or another all the time. We are constantly bombarded with advertisements and messaging that are carefully tailored to us. Some want us to buy a particular type of jeans or drink a certain soft drink. Others want us to change our job, support a good cause or start a new work-out regime. Where do we draw the line between advertisement and manipulation? The only thing separating the two is the strength of the algorithm, isn't it?

### Fake news!

The 2016 presidential election in the US created fake news stories that were often produced by propaganda websites and subsequently spread via social media.

We have always had news sites with a certain political leaning which to a greater or lesser degree coloured its coverage, but what we saw in the 2016 election was a flurry of entirely fabricated news stories created for the purpose of misinformation and to create confusion.

In the same way as fake news was created in order to fabricate an alternative reality to the one described in the traditional news sources, so Outside Insight can also expect to see its fair share of fake breadcrumbs produced by companies that want to confuse and outmanoeuvre their competitors. As Outside Insight becomes increasingly widespread, such fake breadcrumbs will become more and more commonplace and will be used by companies to hide their real intentions. This will induce an arms race between those who are producing fake breadcrumbs and those who can identify them. This arms race will be very similar to what we today see between those who create viruses and those who create anti-virus software.

## The beginning of a new era

It is the nature of all new technologies to solve problems that could not be solved before and at the same time inadvertently create new problems for which we have to find good solutions. Outside Insight is no exception in this respect.

The three problems that are outlined above – how we protect people's privacy, how we make sure our algorithms are ethical, or are used ethically, and how we address the natural development of fake breadcrumbs – are all important areas of concern. I don't have immediate solutions. All I want to do is to raise awareness of the issues. As we scramble to implement Outside Insight solutions, I also think it is important that we are mindful of the ethical issues that will come up so that we can find ways to tackle them. Only then can we fully benefit from all the benefits Outside Insight has to offer.

# Chapter Seventeen

# The Future of Outside Insight

We live in a world drowning in data. Our interactions with each other and with the world around us take place increasingly through digital means: our mobile phones, our web browsers, our email accounts, our social media accounts and our messaging apps. The more we convert to digital, the more data we produce. As individuals and as companies, we all leave behind digital breadcrumbs.

In this book we have discussed how these breadcrumbs are largely overlooked at present. We have discussed how this is a big missed opportunity and how analysis of online breadcrumbs can be beneficial for boards, executives, marketers, product developers, risk managers and investors.

Although Outside Insight is in its infancy today, its significance should not be underestimated. Companies that embrace Outside Insight will make decisions with an information advantage and over time will outperform peers who don't. For this reason Outside Insight will become a core, indispensable tool for managers across every business function.

The adoption of Oracle, CRM, BI and ERP shaped modern management into a rigorous data-driven practice based on internal data. The adoption of Outside Insight will have a similar effect, this time for external data. As technology and software catch up with the complexity of harvesting the open internet for valuable insights, Outside Insight will become as commonplace as BI and CRM are today and quickly become one of the most important tools in the next-generation management toolbox.

The adoption of Outside Insight will dramatically alter how companies are governed and run. It will introduce a new transparency in the boardroom and will transform decision-making from being reactive to being proactive, and executives will shift their focus from operational efficiency to a holistic understanding of the ebb and flow of their industry.

## A new transparency in the boardroom

As a board member, it is often difficult to understand fully what is going on within the operational side of the business. The board has to go by what is presented to it by the management. Management presents a narrative supported by data and analysis, but their outlook will inevitably be coloured by their personal beliefs and motives.

By incorporating Outside Insight, it is possible to assess a company's performance based on third-party data. Through an apples-to-apples comparison with industry peers it is possible to understand how well a company is developing independently of management reports and beliefs.

By bringing Outside Insight into the boardroom, the board can determine how well a company is performing compared with its competitors along critical, forward-looking dimensions. This will inevitably change the conversation. Rather than spending time looking at historical data, the board can evaluate strategic questions such as: what is the size and sentiment of our online brand footprint? Is it trending positively or negatively compared with our competitors? Which company has the happiest clients? How has this trended the last twelve months? How much are we investing in sales and marketing? Do we invest below or above the industry average?

Such analysis will never be able to replace management reports, but it will give the board an invaluable understanding of overall industry trends. Introducing Outside Insight into the boardroom provides board members with a valuable backdrop to interpret management reports and to engage in constructive boardroom discussions.

In between board meetings, board members can access real-time Outside Insight dashboards to help them keep a finger on the pulse of the industry.

## *The transition from reactive to proactive*

Business practices today rely heavily on internal data such as financials, but making decisions based on historic financial results is a very reactive approach to running a company. Company financials are the end-result of investments and activities that took place in the past. To study the financials is to study the aftermath of historical events.

The future results of a company are a function of its ability to retain existing business and to compete for new. Central to a company's ability to compete, therefore, is a deep understanding of how the competitive dynamics in the market-place are changing.

With Outside Insight, changes to the competitive dynamics can be detected in real time. Outside Insight provides forward-looking information with many clues to how a company's competitiveness will develop. Client satisfaction, advertising expenditure and job postings are all examples of this. Client satisfaction can be analysed in real time, and its trend can be prescriptive of future churn or new client wins. If competitors are increasing their ad spend, it signals future increased competitive pressure. Job postings are early indications of investments and can signal whether competitors are investing in sales or product development.

Moving from analysis of internal data to Outside Insight is a transformation from a reactive to proactive decision paradigm. Lagging performance indicators such as financials are replaced by real-time analysis flagging new threats and opportunities in the competitive landscape. Long-term sustained success is ensured by taking action proactively and decisively when changes in market and conditions arise.

## From operational efficiency to industry overview

Internal data is about your company. A focus on internal data fosters an inwardly focused culture of operational efficiency. Transitioning to external data is replacing the operational tunnel vision with a peripheral vision to study the ebb and flow of the overall industry.

The Outside Insight emphasis on a good command of external market conditions does not necessarily contradict a focus on operational efficiency. Well-positioned companies often play to their strengths and achieve high operational efficiency as a result. With the Outside Insight approach, though, the external factors are always centre-stage because it doesn't matter that a company operates like a well-oiled machine if the market-place is changing and rendering the company irrelevant.

Outside Insight acknowledges that a company's future depends on more than just internal factors and that it exists within a broader ecosystem. A company is influenced by a large range of external factors, and executives need to develop a deep understanding of these in order to be conscientious and successful stewards of their company.

## The long-term impact of Outside Insight

The positive impacts of Outside Insight in the short to medium term are pretty straightforward. Executives will make more informed decisions because new types of information will be included in the decision-making process. By understanding real-time trends in external factors, executives will also become more responsive to changes in their market-place.

In the long run, the impact of Outside Insight will become much more profound and will be hard to overstate. There are three macro trends driving this development: exponential growth of cloud-based computing power, exponential advances in artificial intelligence and exponential growth of external data. Together these trends will converge to create Outside Insight software with staggering capabilities.

In the future the job of an executive will look very different from the way it looks today. Decisions will no longer be based on data points and insights, but will be guided instead by prediction of future outcomes with the help of AI, game theory and scenario analysis.

In the future, an executive will be supported by an abundance of computation power and powerful AI. Any potential decision will be carefully analysed and scored by large computer clusters processing historical and up-to-the-second intelligence about competitors and other players in the ecosystem. Competitors' possible counter-moves will be listed in order of probability and rated by corresponding positive and negative consequences.

Data analysis will at this point be completely automated. The Outside Insight software will be the sensory interface with the external world, and the internal ERP systems will be the feedback loops of gains and losses of decisions made. The Outside Insight brain, consisting of all its artificial intelligence, will be the oracle that scenario analysis managers, executives, boards and investors will consult.

## A new era

As the world moves further down the digital path, as machines become increasingly intelligent and data science increasingly more sophisticated, Outside Insight will make a profound impact and completely change the way we think of corporate strategy and decision-making.

Outside Insight has the potential to transform dramatically the way companies are governed and run. Outside

Insight has the potential to transform dramatically what it will take to become a successful business executive.

After Outside Insight business will not be the same.

It's time to enter the front lines of a new era.

It's time to embrace change.

# Appendix: Outside Insight Complimentary Licence

Complimentary with the first edition of the *Outside Insight* book is a licence to a limited version of Meltwater's Outside Insight app. The app creates a report on your competitive health based on Outside Insight. It benchmarks you against your competitors in four default arenas of competitive tension. These are: strength of brand, client satisfaction, online ad spend and hiring momentum. The app also comes with an anomaly detection feature, which triggers real-time alerts if it detects unusual patterns.

| Competitive arena | How it is measured | Measurement |
|---|---|---|
| Strength of brand | Measures the strength and size of your online footprint. The key drivers will be mentions in news and social media. Sentiment is carefully assessed to understand whether media mentions are advantageous or not. | Net number of people you have touched with a positive sentiment. |
| Client satisfaction | Measures the social media feedback on your products and services. | The percentage of feedback you receive through social media that is positive. |
| Online ad spend | The default licence estimates spend on the Google search engine. | Money spent on Google's ad spend. |
| Hiring | Tracks the hiring pattern that is announced in the public domain. | Number of new hires. |

The app can be downloaded by going to www. outsideinsight.com/app. By using the one-time code found on the jacket of this book, you can activate your complimentary three-month licence. There is currently only support for iOS, but there is also a web version available until the Android version is released.

The complimentary Outside Insight app offered to readers of this book is a stripped-down version of Meltwater's solution. This comes with a lot of room for customization as well as analytics on a wide range of additional data. The premium solution also offers the opportunity to import proprietary data sources.

Although the complimentary licence available to readers of this book is a light version of Meltwater's software, it is nevertheless a good way to dip your toe into the world of Outside Insight and see how it can be used in practice to understand a company's competitive landscape and to anticipate future opportunities and threats.

In the remainder of this Appendix the analysis provided by the complimentary licence is explained in more detail.

### Company brand

The company brand analysis consists of two pages and eight panes of analyses showing how you are sitting in your industry compared with your peers.

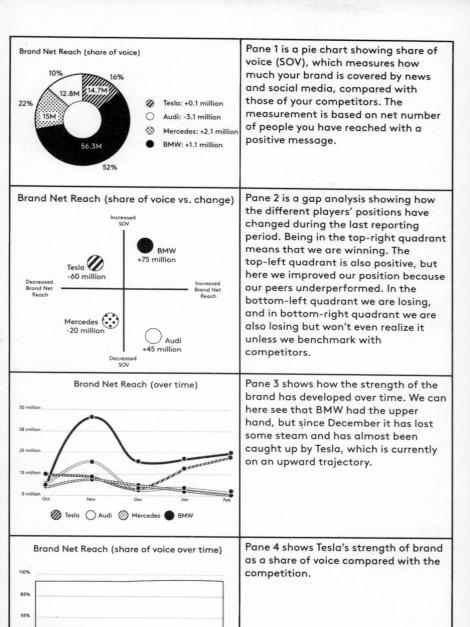

**Brand Net Reach (share of voice)**

- Tesla: +0.1 million
- Audi: -3.1 million
- Mercedes: +2.1 million
- BMW: +1.1 million

16%
10%
14.7M
12.8M
22%
15M
56.3M
52%

Pane 1 is a pie chart showing share of voice (SOV), which measures how much your brand is covered by news and social media, compared with those of your competitors. The measurement is based on net number of people you have reached with a positive message.

**Brand Net Reach (share of voice vs. change)**

Increased SOV

BMW +75 million

Tesla -60 million

Decreased Brand Net Reach — Increased Brand Net Reach

Mercedes -20 million

Audi +45 million

Decreased SOV

Pane 2 is a gap analysis showing how the different players' positions have changed during the last reporting period. Being in the top-right quadrant means that we are winning. The top-left quadrant is also positive, but here we improved our position because our peers underperformed. In the bottom-left quadrant we are losing, and in bottom-right quadrant we are also losing but won't even realize it unless we benchmark with competitors.

**Brand Net Reach (over time)**

50 million
38 million
25 million
13 million
0 million
Oct Nov Dec Jan Feb

Tesla  Audi  Mercedes  BMW

Pane 3 shows how the strength of the brand has developed over time. We can here see that BMW had the upper hand, but since December it has lost some steam and has almost been caught up by Tesla, which is currently on an upward trajectory.

**Brand Net Reach (share of voice over time)**

110%
83%
55%
28%
0%
Oct Nov Dec Jan Feb

Tesla  Rest of Group

Pane 4 shows Tesla's strength of brand as a share of voice compared with the competition.

The next four panes provide further drill-down analyses to get a better understanding of your company's brand and that of your competitors.

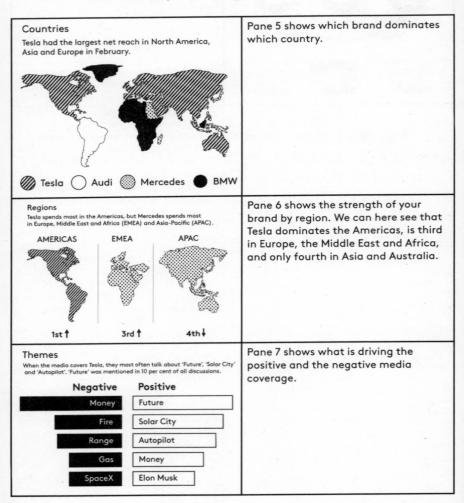

**Countries**

Tesla had the largest net reach in North America, Asia and Europe in February.

Tesla / Audi / Mercedes / BMW

Pane 5 shows which brand dominates which country.

**Regions**

Tesla spends most in the Americas, but Mercedes spends most in Europe, Middle East and Africa (EMEA) and Asia-Pacific (APAC).

AMERICAS    EMEA    APAC

1st ↑    3rd ↑    4th ↓

Pane 6 shows the strength of your brand by region. We can here see that Tesla dominates the Americas, is third in Europe, the Middle East and Africa, and only fourth in Asia and Australia.

**Themes**

When the media covers Tesla, they most often talk about 'Future', 'Solar City' and 'Autopilot'. 'Future' was mentioned in 10 per cent of all discussions.

| Negative | Positive |
|---|---|
| Money | Future |
| Fire | Solar City |
| Range | Autopilot |
| Gas | Money |
| SpaceX | Elon Musk |

Pane 7 shows what is driving the positive and the negative media coverage.

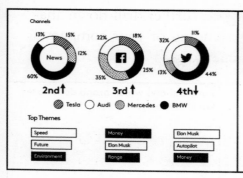

Pane 8 shows your brand's strength in news, on Facebook and on Twitter. Rankings as well as dominating positive and negative themes are also highlighted.

The other three dimensions are built up with the same logic. First there are four panes with an overall trend analysis comparing your development with your competition. The last four panes provide a drill-down to help you better understand why things have developed as they have and what you can do to improve your position.

# Acknowledgements

This book would never have come to life without the help and constant support from a lot of people. I have to start by thanking my editors, Daniel Crewe and Keith Taylor from Penguin Random House. Thank you for all your support. I greatly appreciate your patience with a multitasking entrepreneur to the very end.

This book would never have been more than an idea without the loving help and contributions from Elen Lewis and Greg Williams. You have worked so hard to make the case studies come to life as well as to mentor me through the emotional roller coaster it is to write a book for the first time. You have been true partners to me from day one and I cannot thank you enough.

Key members of Team Outside Insight are the wonderful people that worked on the manuscript edits, illustrations, jacket design, website, companion app, and promotion. Under the diligent oversight of Natasha Nissar and Thea Sokolowski, this has been executed with military precision. Natasha has been one of my closest colleagues for many years, and she never ceases to amaze me with her ability to juggle a million balls without losing her cool. Thank you for being such an amazing, graceful person and daily inspiration. Thea Sokolowski came in as a whirlwind towards the latter part of the project and brought everything over the finishing line, against all odds. Thank you to Nick Acosta for the beautiful illustrations. Thank you to Ursula Tereba for all the research work. Thank you to Camy Anguile for always being there for support and administration.

The Meltwater Labs team also deserves a big shout out. Spearheaded by Chad Hamre and Robert Rydefalk, this team has worked tirelessly to create Meltwater's first OI app. When it comes to promotion of the book I am deeply indebted to Matt Michelsen, who is the most generous and supportive guy you can have on your team. My partner Victoria Haynes has not been an official member of team Outside Insight, but has been my biggest supporter and advisor from day one. Thank you, Victoria, for your constant encouragement and support through countless evenings, weekends, and vacations.

A number of people have supported me by providing feedback to earlier manuscripts. Thank you for your time and for your honest feedback. In no particular order, I would like to thank Dag Opdal, Harald Berg, Rainer Gawlick, Harald Mix, Matt Blodgett, Vincent Kouvenhowen, Matt Michelsen, Brian Flynn, Adam Jackson, Chris Regester, Ajay Khari, Andy Ann, Chad Hamre, Robert Rydefalk, Nick Couch, Affan Butt, Jeff Epstein, Gary Briggs, C. S. Park, John Burbank, Joe Lonsdale, Peter Tufano, Kathy Harvey, Oliver Guinness, Sang Kim, Ragnhild Silkoset, Brian Seth, Jim Davidson, and Larry Sonsini.

Finally, I would also like to take the opportunity to

thank my colleagues at Meltwater. When Gard Haugen and I started the business back in the day and were later joined by Jens Petter Glittenberg, it was a pretty humble undertaking, and I find it quite astonishing that so many amazing people decided to join us in spite of how little we had to show. Thank you to everybody in Meltwater past and present. Thank you for believing in this small Norwegian startup and for all your hard work and contributions. A special thank you to Meltwater veterans Paal Larsen, Niklas de Besche, Kaveh Rostampor, John Box, Mike Ruggieri, Marty Hernandez, Jonas Oppedal, Hanna Orquist, Kevin Lorenz, and Mirjam Engebretsen. The inspiration for this book is a direct result of all our hard work, all our learnings, and all our dreams. I cannot thank you enough for the amazing journey we have had together. I could not have had better colleagues. Or a better time. For both I will always be deeply grateful.

# Sources

## *Introduction*

1 Jordan Novet, 'Apple Has Laid off All of Its Contract Recruiters, Source Says', VentureBeat, 25 Apr. 2016.
2 Emil Protalinski, 'Apple Sees IPhone Sales Fall for the First Time: Down 16.3% to 51.2 Million in Q2 2016', VentureBeat, 26 Apr. 2016.

## *Chapter 1. Everyone Leaves Online Breadcrumbs*

1 Owen Mundy, 'About "I Know Where Your Cat Lives"', iknowwhereyourcatlives.com/about.
2 Kimberlee Morrison, 'How Many Photos Are Uploaded to Snapchat Every Second?', *Adweek*, 9 June 2015.
3 Mary Meeker, '2016 Internet Trends', Kleiner Perkins Caufield Byers, 1 June 2016.
4 Worldometers' RTS Algorithm. 'Twitter Usage Statistics', Twitter Usage Statistics. Internet Live Stats, n.d. <http://www.internetlivestats.com/twitter-statistics/>.
5 Kit Smith, '47 Incredible Facebook Statistics and Facts for 2016', Brandwatch, 12 May 2016. <https://www.brandwatch.com/blog/47-facebook-statistics-2016/>.
6 Kyle Brigham, '10 Facts About YouTube That Will Blow Your Mind', Linkedin Pulse, 26 Feb. 2015. <https://www.linkedin.com/pulse/10-facts-youtube-blow-your-mind-kyle-brigham>.

7 Chester Jesus Soria, 'NYPD Bust Alleged Gang Rivalry between Harlem Housing Projects', *NY Metro*, 4 June 2014.

8 Cyrus R. Vance Jr, 'District Attorney Vance and Police Commissioner Bratton Announce Largest Indicted Gang Case in NYC History', The New York County District Attorney's Office, 4 June 2014.

9 Alice Speri, 'The Kids Arrested in the Largest Gang Bust in NYC History Got Caught Because of Facebook', VICE News, 5 June 2014.

10 'US Digital Display Ad Spending to Surpass Search Ad Spending in 2016', eMarketer, 11 Jan. 2016. <https://www.emarketer.com/Article/US-Digital-Display-Ad-Spending-Surpass-Search-Ad-Spending-2016/1013442>.

11 'AAPL Historical Prices/Apple Inc. Stock: 1987–1998', Yahoo! Finance.

12 Dawn Kawamoto, 'Microsoft to Invest $150 Million in Apple', CNET, 6 Jan. 2009.

13 Verne Kopytoff, 'Apple: The First $700 Billion Company.' Fortune, 10 Feb. 2015. <http://fortune.com/2015/02/10/apple-the-first-700-billion-company/>.

## *Chapter 2. Mining Internal Data Is Looking at the Past*

1 'ORCL Annual Income Statement', Annual Financials for Oracle Corp., MarketWatch. <http://www.marketwatch.com/investing/stock/orcl/financials>.

2 William Brown and Frank Nasuti, 'What ERP Systems Can Tell Us about Sarbanes-Oxley'. *Information Management & Computer Security*, 13.4: 311–27. doi: 10.1108/09685220510614434.

3 'Gartner Says Worldwide IT Spending Is Forecast to Grow 0.6 Percent in 2016', Gartner, 18 Jan. 2016. <http://www.gartner.com/newsroom/id/3186517>.

4 'Q4 FY16 SaaS and PaaS Revenues Were Up 66%, and Up 68% in Constant Currency', Oracle Financial News, 16 June 2016. <http://investor.oracle.com/financial-news/financial-news-details/2016/Q4-FY16-SaaS-and-PaaS-Revenues-Were-Up-66-and-Up-68-in-Constant-Currency/default.aspx>.

5 Babson College, 'Welcome from the Dean'. <http://www.babson.edu/program/graduate/Pages/dean-message.aspx>, accessed 24 January 2014.

6 Jacquie McNish and Sean Silcoff, *Losing the Signal: The Untold Story behind the Extraordinary Rise and Spectacular Fall of BlackBerry*. New York: Flatiron, 2016.

7 'RIM's (BlackBerry) Market Share 2007–2016, by Quarter', Statista. <https://www.statista.com/statistics/263439/global-market-share-held-by-rim-smartphones/>.

8 Andrea Hopkins and Alastair Sharp, 'RIM CEO Says "Nothing Wrong" with BlackBerry Maker', Reuters, 3 July 2012. <http://www.reuters.com/article/us-rim-ceo-IDUSBRE8620NL20120703>.

9 Brad Reed, 'BlackBerry Announces Major Job Cuts, Quarterly Net Operating Loss of $1 Billion', BGR Media, 20 Sept. 2013. <http://bgr.com/2013/09/20/blackberry-layoffs-announcement/>.

10 Jacquie McNish and Sean Silcoff, 'The Inside Story of How the iPhone Crippled BlackBerry', *Wall Street Journal*, 22 May 2015. <https://www.wsj.com/articles/behind-the-rise-and-fall-of-blackberry-1432311912>.

## Chapter 3. Mining External Data Is
## Looking into the Future

1 'RaceTrac Petroleum on the Forbes America's Largest Private Companies List', *Forbes*, 30 Apr. 2016.

2 'The History of Kodak', *Wall Street Journal*, 3 Oct. 2011. <https://www.wsj.com/news/articles/SB1000142405297 02041382045766050423627706666>.

3 Steve Hamm and William C. Symonds, 'Mistakes Made on the Road to Innovation', Bloomberg.com, 26 Nov. 2006. <https://www.bloomberg.com/news/articles/2006-11-26/mistakes-made-on-the-road-to-innovation>.

4 Kamal Munir, 'The Demise of Kodak: Five Reasons', *Wall Street Journal*, 26 Feb. 2012. <http://blogs.wsj.com/source/2012/02/26/the-demise-of-kodak-five-reasons/>.

5 Sue Zeidler, 'Kodak Sells Online Business to Shutterfly', Reuters, 2 Mar. 2012. <http://www.reuters.com/article/us-kodak-shutterfly-IDUSTRE8202AY20120302>.

6 M. G. Siegler, 'Burbn's Funding Goes Down Smooth. Baseline, Andreessen Back Stealthy Location Startup', TechCrunch, 5 Mar. 2010.

7 M. G. Siegler, 'Instagram Filters through Suitors to Capture $7 Million in Funding Led by Benchmark', TechCrunch, 2 Feb. 2011.

8 'The Instagram Community – Ten Million and Counting', Instagram, 26 Sept. 2011. <http://blog.instagram.com/post/10692926832/10million>.

9 Bonnie Cha, 'Apple Names Instagram iPhone App of the Year', CNET, 8 Dec. 2011. <https://www.cnet.com/uk/news/apple-names-instagram-iphone-app-of-the-year/>.

10 Alexia Tsotsis, 'Right before Acquisition, Instagram Closed $50M at a $500M Valuation From Sequoia, Thrive, Greylock And Benchmark', TechCrunch, 9 Apr. 2012.

11 Dan Primack, 'Breaking: Facebook Buying Instagram for $1 Billion', Fortune, 9 Apr. 2012. <http://fortune.com/2012/04/09/breaking-facebook-buying-instagram-for-1-billion/>.

12 Kim-Mai Cutler, 'Instagram Reaches 27 Million Registered Users and Says Its Android App Is Nearly Here', TechCrunch, 11 Mar. 2012. <https://techcrunch.com/2012/03/11/instagram-reaches-27-million-registered-users-shows-off-upcoming-android-app/>.

13 Dan Farber, 9 May 2012 3:38 am, BST. 'Zuckerberg Takes Heat for Hoodie on IPO Road Show', CNET, 8 May 2012. <https://www.cnet.com/uk/news/zuckerberg-takes-heat-for-hoodie-on-ipo-road-show/>.

14 Jillian D'Onfro, 'Mark Mahaney: How Facebook Is Taking Over the World', Business Insider, 9 Dec. 2015. <http://uk.businessinsider.com/mark-mahaney-rbc-capital-markets-presentation-on-facebook-2015-12?r=US&IR=T%2F#here-are-the-four-biggest-opportunities-ahead-9>.

15 Maya Kosoff, 'Here's How Two Analysts Think Instagram Could Be Worth up to $37 Billion', Business Insider, 16 Mar. 2015. <http://uk.businessinsider.com/instagram-valuation-2015-3?r=US&IR=T>.

## Chapter 4. Outside Insight: A New Decision
## Paradigm for a New Digital Reality

1 'Life Onboard', Volvo Ocean Race Press Zone, 29 Aug. 2014. <http://www.volvooceanrace.com/en/presszone/en/29_Life-onboard.html>.

2 Eugene Platon, 'Volvo Ocean Race 2014–15 Media Report',Issuu, 2 Dec. 2015. <https://issuu.com/eugene_platon/docs/volvo_ocean_race_2014-15_race_repor>.

3 'Worldwide IT Software Spending 2009-2020', Statista. <https://www.statista.com/statistics/203428/total-enterprise-software-revenue-forecast/>.

4 'Media Intelligence and Public Relations Information & Software Spend Topped USD2.6 Billion in 2014, Up 7.12%', Burton-Taylor International Consulting, 28 Apr. 2015. <https://burton-taylor.com/media-intelligence-and-public-relations-information-software-spend-topped-usd2-6-billion-in-2014-up-7-12-3/>.

5 'Number of Registered Hike Messenger Users from February 2014 to January 2016', Statista. <https://www.statista.com/statistics/348738/hike-messenger-registered-users/>.

6 Parmy Olson, 'Facebook Closes $19 Billion WhatsApp Deal', *Forbes Magazine*, 6 Oct. 2014. <http://www.forbes.com/sites/parmyolson/2014/10/06/facebook-closes-19-billion-whatsapp-deal/#7a3e843c179e>.

7 Jon Russell, 'India's WhatsApp Rival Hike Raises $175M Led by Tencent at a $1.4B valuation', TechCrunch, 16 Aug. 2016. <https://techcrunch.com/2016/08/16/indias-whatsapp-rival-hike-raises-175m-led-by-tencent-at-a-1-4b-valuation/>.

## Chapter 5: The Value of External Data

1 Michael Lewis and Jonas Karlsson, 'Betting on the Blind Side', *Vanity Fair*, 24 Sept. 2015. <http://www.vanityfair. com/news/2010/04/wall-street-excerpt-201004>.

2 'The State of the Nation's Housing', Joint Center for Housing Studies of Harvard University. <http://www.jchs. harvard.edu/sites/jchs.harvard.edu/files/son2008.pdf>. See Figure 4, p. 4.

3 Roger C. Altman, 'The Great Crash, 2008', *Foreign Affairs*, 3 Feb. 2009. <https://www.foreignaffairs.com/articles/ united-states/2009-01-01/great-crash-2008>.

4 Steve Blumenthal, 'On My Radar: Global Recession a High Probability', CMG, 20 Nov. 2015. <http://www. cmgwealth.com/ri/on-my-radar-glgh-probability/>.

5 Michael J. Burry, 'I Saw the Crisis Coming. Why Didn't the Fed?' *The New York Times*, 4 Apr. 2010. <http://www. nytimes.com/2010/04/04/opinion/04burry.html>.

6 Tyler Durden, 'Profiling "The Big Short's" Michael Burry', Zero Hedge, 20 July 2011. <http://www.zero hedge.com/article/profiling-big-shorts-michael-burry>.

7 Robert Peston, 'Northern Rock Gets Bank Bail Out', BBC News, 13 Sept. 2007. <http://news.bbc.co.uk/1/hi/business/ 6994099.stm>.

8 Paul Sims and Sean Poulter, 'Northern Rock: Business-man Barricades in Branch Manager for Refusing to Give Him £1 Million Savings', *Daily Mail*, 15 Sept. 2007. <http://www.mailonsunday.co.uk/news/article-481852/ Northern-Rock-Businessman-barricades-branch-manager-refusing-1-million-savings.html>.

9 David Lawder, 'U.S. Backs Away from Plan to Buy Bad Assets', Reuters, 12 Nov. 2008. <http://www.reuters.com/article/us-financial-paulson-IDUSTRE4AB7P820081112>.

10 'JPMorgan Chase and Bear Stearns Announce Amended Merger Agreement and Agreement for JPMorgan Chase to Purchase 39.5% of Bear Stearns', SEC, 24 Mar. 2008. <https://www.sec.gov/Archives/edgar/data/19617/0000 89882208000320/pressrelease.htm>.

11 'A.I.G.'s $85 Billion Government Bailout', The New York Times, 17 Sept. 2008. <https://dealbook.nytimes.com/2008/09/17/aigs-85-billion-government-bailout/>.

12 'Case Study: The Collapse of Lehman Brothers', Investopedia, 16 Feb. 2017. <http://www.investopedia.com/articles/economics/09/lehman-brothers-collapse.asp>.

13 Steve Fishman, 'Burning Down His House', New York, 30 Nov. 2008. <http://nymag.com/news/business/52603/>.

14 David Ellis, 'Lehman Posts $2.8 Billion Loss', Cable News Network, 9 June 2008. <http://money.cnn.com/2008/06/09/news/companies/lehman_results/>.

## Chapter 6. The Value of Real Time

1 Richard Pallardy and John P. Rafferty, 'Chile Earthquake of 2010', Encyclopædia Britannica, 4 May 2016. <https://www.britannica.com/event/Chile-Earthquake-of-2010>.

2 https://twitter.com/AlarmaSismos.

3 Amanda Coleman, 'A New Type of Emergency Plan', Corp-Comms, 10 Jan. 2011. <http://www.corpcommsmagazine.co.uk/features/1694-a-new-type-of-emergency-plan>.

4 Dom Phillips, 'Brazil's Mining Tragedy: Was It a Preventable Disaster?', The Guardian, 25 Nov. 2015. <https://www.

theguardian.com/sustainable-business/2015/nov/25/
brazils-mining-tragedy-dam-preventable-disaster-samarco-
vale-bhp-billiton>.

5 'Deadly Dam Burst in Brazil Prompts Calls for Stricter
Mining Regulations', *The Guardian*, 10 Nov. 2015. <https://
www.theguardian.com/world/2015/nov/10/brazil-dam-
burst-mining-rules>.

6 Duane Stanford, 'Coke Engineers Its Orange Juice – With
an Algorithm', Bloomberg, 31 Jan. 2013. <https://www.
bloomberg.com/news/articles/2013-01-31/coke-engineers-
its-orange-juice-with-an-algorithm>.

7 'Walmart Announces Q4 Underlying EPS of $1.61 and
Additional Strategic Investments in People & e-Commerce;
Walmart U.S. Comp Sales Increased 1.5 Percent', Walmart
Corporate. <http://corporate.walmart.com/_news_/news-
archive/investors/2015/02/19/walmart-announces-q4-
underlying-eps-of-161-and-additional-strategic-investments-
in-people-e-commerce-walmart-us-comp-sales-increased-
15-percent>.

8 'Data, Data Everywhere', *The Economist*, 27 Feb. 2010.
<http://www.economist.com/node/15557443>.

9 Pascal-Emmanuel Gobry, 'Why Walmart Spent $300 Million
on a Social Media Startup', Business Insider, 19 Apr. 2011.
<http://www.businessinsider.com/heres-why-walmart-
spent-300-million-on-a-social-media-startup-2011-4?IR=T>.

10 Flightcompensation.com.

11 Lily Newman, 'Algorithm Improves Airline Arrival Predictions, Erodes Favourite Work Excuse', Gizmodo UK, 7
Apr. 2013. <http://www.gizmodo.co.uk/2013/04/algorithm-
improves-airline-arrival-predictions-erodes-favorite-work-
excuse/>.

## Chapter 7. The Value of Benchmarking

1 Matt Marshall, 'They Did It! YouTube Bought by Google for $1.65B in Less than Two Years', VentureBeat, 9 Oct. 2006. <http://venturebeat.com/2006/10/09/they-did-it-youtube-gets-bought-by-gooogle-for-165b-in-less-than-two-years/>.

2 Robert C. Camp, *Benchmarking: The Search for Industry Best Practices That Lead to Superior Performance*. University Park, IL: Productivity, 2007.

3 Felipe Thomaz, Andrew T. Stephen and Vanitha Swaminathan, 'Using Social Media Monitoring Data to Forecast Online Word-of-Mouth Valence: A Network Autoregressive Approach', Said Business School Research Papers, Sept. 2015. <http://eureka.sbs.ox.ac.uk/5842/1/2015-15.pdf>.

4 Frances X. Frei and Corey B. Hajim, 'Commerce Bank', Harvard Business School, Case 603-080, December 2002 (revised October 2006). <http://www.hbs.edu/faculty/Pages/item.aspx?num=29457>.

5 United States Postal Service, 'Postal Facts 2015', USPS, 2015. <https://about.usps.com/who-we-are/postal-facts/postalfacts2015.pdf>.

6 Phil Rosenthal, 'A Love Letter: The U.S. Postal Service Delivers under Tough Conditions', *Chicago Tribune*, 18 Jan. 2015. <http://www.chicagotribune.com/business/columnists/ct-rosenthal-us-mail-post-office-0118-biz-2015 0117-column.html>.

## Chapter 8. Outside Insight for Boards and Executives

1 Matthew J. Belvedere, 'Caterpillar CEO: Big Misses Reflect "rough Patch"', CNBC, 22 Oct. 2015. <http://www.cnbc.com/2015/10/22/caterpillar-earnings-revenue-miss-expectation.html>.

2 Kylie Dumble, 'The KPMG Survey of Environmental Reporting: 1997', KPMG, 2014. <https://assets.kpmg.com/content/dam/kpmg/pdf/2014/06/kpmg-survey-business-reporting.pdf>.

3 Martin Reeves, Claire Love and Philipp Tillmanns, 'Your Strategy Needs a Strategy', *Harvard Business Review*, September 2012.

4 Jim Edwards, 'We Finally Got Some Really Good Data on Just How Much Money Google Makes from YouTube and Google Play', Business Insider, 10 July 2015. <http://uk.businessinsider.com/stats-on-googles-revenues-from-youtube-and-google-play-2015-7?r=US&IR=T>.

## Chapter 9. Outside Insight for Marketers

1 'Guinness World Records', Wikipedia, 22 Feb. 2017. <https://en.wikipedia.org/wiki/Guinness_World_Records>.

2 World Bank.

3 CIA World Factbook.

4 'Duck and Run', *The Economist*, 12 Aug. 2009. <http://www.economist.com/node/14207217>.

5 Sasha Issenberg, 'How Obama Used Big Data to Rally Voters, Part 1', *MIT Technology Review*, 20 Mar. 2014. <https://www.technologyreview.com/s/508836/how-obama-used-big-data-to-rally-voters-part-1/>

6 Niall McCarthy, 'How Much Does Money Matter in U.S. Presidential Elections?', *Forbes Magazine*, 28 July 2016. <http://www.forbes.com/sites/niallmccarthy/2016/07/28/how-much-does-money-matter-in-u-s-presidential-elections-infographic/#6a5f69a97c14>

7 Michael Scherer, 'How Obama's Data Crunchers Helped Him Win', Cable News Network, 7 Nov. 2012. <http://edition.cnn.com/2012/11/07/tech/web/obama-campaign-tech-team/>

8 '2014 State of B2B Procurement Study: Uncovering the Shifting Landscape in B2B Commerce', Accenture, 24 June 2015. <https://www.accenture.com/t20150624T211502__w__/us-en/_acnmedia/Accenture/Conversion-Assets/DotCom/Documents/Global/PDF/Industries_15/Accenture-B2B-Procurement-Study.pdf>.

9 Stephen Pulvirent, 'How Daniel Wellington Made a $200 Million Business out of Cheap Watches', Bloomberg, 14 July 2015. <https://www.bloomberg.com/news/articles/2015-07-14/how-daniel-wellington-made-a-200-million-business-out-of-cheap-watches>.

10 Kara Lawson, 'Shareablee Exclusive Series: Daniel Wellington Watches', Shareablee Blog, 8 June 2015. <http://blog.shareablee.com/shareablee-exclusive-series-daniel-wellington-watches>.

11 James O'Malley, 'How to Get a One Plus One Phone without an Invite', Tech. Digest, 9 Feb. 2015. <http://www.techdigest.tv/2015/02/how-to-get-a-one-plus-one-phone-without-an-invite.html.>.

12 Angela Doland, 'OnePlus: The Startup That Actually Convinced People To Smash Their iPhones', *Advertising Age*, 10

Aug. 2015. <http://adage.com/article/cmo-strategy/oneplus-convinced-people-smash-iphones/299875/>.
13 Patrick Barkham, 'Zip Up, Look Sharp: The OnePiece Roadtested', *Guardian*, 26 Nov. 2010. <https://www.the guardian.com/lifeandstyle/2010/nov/26/onepiece-mens-fashion>.
14 'OnePiece Story & Legacy', OnePiece, n.d. <https://www.onepiece.co.uk/en-gb/onepiece>.
15 https://twitter.com/onepiece/status/536575565567127552.

## Chapter 10. Outside Insight for Product Development

1 Jeff Prosise, 'The Netscape Security Breach', *PC Magazine*, 23 Apr. 1996.
2 'Netscape Announces "Netscape Bugs Bounty" with Release of Netscape Navigator 2.0 Beta', Netscape, 10 Oct. 1995. <http://web.archive.org/web/19970501041756/www101.netscape.com/newsref/pr/newsrelease48.html>.
3 J. Donald Fernie, 'The Harrison-Maskelyne Affair', *American Scientist*, Oct. 2003. <http://www.americanscientist.org/issues/pub/2003/5/the-harrison-maskelyne-affair>.
4 Vlad Savov, 'The Entire History of IPhone vs. Android Summed Up in Two Charts', The Verge, 1 June 2016. <http://www.theverge.com/2016/6/1/11836816/iphone-vs-android-history-charts>.
5 Marion Debruyne, *Google Books*. London: Kogan Page, 2014.
6 Olivia Solon, 'Fiat Releases Details of First Ever Crowdsourced Car', *WIRED*, 23 May 2016. <http://www.wired.co.uk/article/fiat-mio>.

7 'A Global Innovation Jam', IBM, n.d. <http://www-03.ibm. com/ibm/history/ibm100/us/en/icons/innovationjam/>.

8 Richard Bak, *The Big Jump: Lindbergh and the Great Atlantic Air Race*. Hoboken, NJ: John Wiley & Sons, 2011.

9 'The Ansari Family', XPRIZE, 19 Apr. 2016. <http:// www.xprize.org/about/vision-circle/ansari-family>.

10 David Leonhardt, 'You Want Innovation? Offer a Prize', *The New York Times*, 30 Jan. 2007. <http://www. nytimes.com/2007/01/31/business/31leonhardt.html>.

11 Alan Boyle, 'Gamers Solve Molecular Puzzle That Baffled Scientists', NBCNews.com, 18 Sept. 2011. <http:// www.nbcnews.com/science/science-news/gamers-solve-molecular-puzzle-baffled-scientists-f6c10402813>.

12 'Two Billion Dollars', Kickstarter, 11 Oct. 2015. <https:// www.kickstarter.com/2billion>.

13 Darrell Etherington, 'Pebble Hits Its $500K Kickstarter Target for Pebble Time in Just 17 Minutes', TechCrunch, 24 Feb. 2015. <https://techcrunch.com/2015/02/24/pebble-hits-its-500k-kickstarter-target-for-pebble-tim-in-just-17-minutes/>.

## Chapter 11. Outside Insight for Risk Management

1 P. D. Darbre, A. Aljarrah, W. R. Miller, N. G. Coldham, M. J. Sauer and G. S. Pope, 'Concentrations of Parabens in Human Breast Tumours', *Journal of Applied Toxicology*, 24.1 (2004): 5–13.

2 'Opinion of the Scientific Committee on Consumer Products on the Safety Evaluation of Parabens', European Commission Health & Consumer Protection Directorate-

General, 28 Jan. 2005. <https://ec.europa.eu/health/ph_risk/committees/04_sccp/docs/sccp_o_019.pdf>.

3 'Restricted Substances List Policy – RB', Reckitt Benckiser, n.d.   <https://www.rb.com/responsibility/policies-and-reports/restricted-substances-list-policy/>.

4 'Palm Oil', Commodities: Palm Oil. Indonesia-investments, 2 Feb. 2016.

5 Belinda Arunarwati Margono, Peter V. Potapov, Svetlana Turubanova, Fred Stolle and Matthew C. Hansen, 'Primary Forest Cover Loss in Indonesia over 2000–2012', *Nature Climate Change*, 4.8 (2014): 730–35.

6 Tim Fernholz, 'What Happens When Apple Finds a Child Making Your iPhone', Quartz, 7 Mar. 2014. <https://qz.com/183563/what-happens-when-apple-finds-a-child-making-your-iphone/>.

7 'HSBC, StanChart to Pay $2.6b US Fines', *Financial Express* [Dhaka], 12 Dec. 2012. <http://print.thefinancialexpress-bd.com/old/index.php?ref=MjBfMTJfMTJfMTJfMV8xXzE1Mjk3Mg>.

8 'HSBC Became Bank to Drug Cartels, Pays Big for Lapses', CNBC, 11 Dec. 2012. <http://www.cnbc.com/id/100303180?view=story&%24DEVICE%24=native-android-mobile>.

9 'Starboard Contacted by Suitors for Yahoo Core Biz', CNBC, 6 Jan. 2016. <http://www.cnbc.com/2016/01/06/starboard-values-ceo-contacted-by-potential-buyers-of-yahoo-core-biz.html?view=story&%24DEVICE%24=native-android-mobile>.

10 Michael J. De La Merced and Vindu Goel, 'Yahoo Agrees to Give 4 Board Seats to Starboard Value', *The New York*

*Times*, 27 Apr. 2016. <https://www.nytimes.com/2016/04/28/business/dealbook/yahoo-board-starboard.html>.

11 Tom DiChristopher, 'Verizon to Acquire Yahoo in $4.8 Billion Deal', CNBC, 25 July 2016. <http://www.cnbc.com/2016/07/25/verizon-to-acquire-yahoo.html>.

12 Stephen Foley and Jennifer Bissell, 'Corporate Governance: The Resurgent Activist', *Financial Times*, 22 June 2014.

### Chapter 12. Outside Insight for Investment Decisions

1 'Akkadian Ventures Closes over $74 Million and Expands Team for Secondary Investing', PR Web, 28 Oct. 2014. <http://www.prweb.com/releases/2014/10/prweb12283611.htm>.

2 Adam Ewing, 'Buyout Fund EQT Starts $632 Million Venture Arm Targeting Europe', Bloomberg, 26 May 2016. <https://www.bloomberg.com/news/articles/2016-05-26/buyout-fund-eqt-starts-632-million-venture-arm-targeting-europe>.

3 Seshadri Tirunillai and Gerard J. Tellis, 'Does Online Chatter Really Matter? Dynamics of User-Generated Content and Stock Performance', 2011. <http://pubsonline.informs.org/doi/abs/10.1287/mksc.1110.0682?journalCode=mksc>.

4 https://www.winton.com/en/

5 Stephen Taub, 'The 2016 Rich List of the World's Top-Earning Hedge Fund Managers', *Institutional Investor's Alpha*, 10 May 2016. <http://www.institutionalinvestorsalpha.com/Article/3552805/The-2016-Rich-List-of-the-Worlds-Top-Earning-Hedge-Fund-Managers.html>.

6 Richard Rubin and Margaret Collins, 'How an Exclusive Hedge Fund Turbocharged Its Retirement Plan', Bloomberg, 16 June 2015. <https://www.bloomberg.com/news/articles/2015-06-16/how-an-exclusive-hedge-fund-turbocharged-retirement-plan>.

7 Nathan Vardi, 'America's Richest Hedge Fund Managers In 2016', *Forbes Magazine*, 4 Oct. 2016. <https://www.forbes.com/sites/nathanvardi/2016/10/04/americas-richest-hedge-fund-managers-in-2016/#6230f9574e2f>.

## Chapter 13. The Emergence of a New Software Category

1 Alex Williams, '$45 Billion Later, Larry Ellison Says No Major Acquisitions For Next Few Years', TechCrunch, 2 Oct. 2012.

2 Margaret Kane, 'Oracle Buys PeopleSoft for $10 Billion', CNET, 13 Dec. 2004. <https://www.cnet.com/uk/news/oracle-buys-peoplesoft-for-10-billion/>.

3 'Oracle Buys NetSuite', Oracle, 28 July 2016. <https://www.oracle.com/corporate/pressrelease/oracle-buys-netsuite-072816.html>.

## Chapter 14. Hard Problems To Solve

1 'New Funding Will Be Used to Expand the Reach of the Predictive Analytics Solution', PRWEB, 9 Mar. 2017. <http://www.wpsdlocal6.com/>.

2 Tomas Kellner, 'Touch Down: GE's Quest to Know When Your Flight Will Land', General Electric, 3 Apr. 2013. <http://www.gereports.com/post/74545138591/touch-down-ges-quest-to-know-when-your-flight/>.

## Chapter 15. New Data Sources

1 William Harwood, 'NASA Launches $855 Million Landsat Mission', CBS News, 11 Feb. 2013. <http://www.cbsnews.com/news/nasa-launches-855-million-landsat-mission/>.

2 Chang-Ran Kim and Kate Holton, 'SoftBank To Buy UK Chip Designer ARM in $32 Billion Cash Deal', Reuters, 18 July 2016. <http://www.reuters.com/article/us-arm-holdings-m-a-softbank-group-IDUSKCN0ZY03B>.

## Chapter 16. The Potential Concerns of Outside Insight

1 Dana Milbank, 'No Matter Who Wins the Presidential Election, Nate Silver Was Right', Washington Post, 8 Nov. 2016.

2 Amanda Cox and Josh Katz, 'Presidential Forecast Post-Mortem', The New York Times, 15 Nov. 2016.

3 Andrew Buncombe, 'AI System That Correctly Predicted Last 3 US Elections Says Donald Trump Will Win', The Independent, 28 Oct. 2016.

4 Hanna Frick, 'Donald Trump Populärast I Sociala Medier', Digitalt. Dagens Media, 8 Nov. 2016. <http://www.dagensmedia.se/medier/digitalt/donald-trump-popularast-i-sociala-medier-6803093>.

5 Sophie Hedestad and Hannes Hultcrantz, 'Meltwater: Så förutsåg vi Brexit', Resumé, 28 June 2016. <https://www.resume.se/nyheter/artiklar/2016/06/28/meltwater-sa-forutsag-vi-brexit/>.

6 Bradley Hope, 'Inside Donald Trump's Data Analytics Team on Election Night', Wall Street Journal, 9 Nov. 2016. <https://

www.wsj.com/articles/inside-donald-trumps-data-analytics-team-on-election-night-1478725225>.

7 Hannes Grassegger and Mikael Krogerus, 'The Data That Turned the World Upside Down', Vice Motherboard, 28 Jan. 2017. <https://motherboard.vice.com/en_us/article/how-our-likes-helped-trump-win>.

8 www.politifact.com/truth-o-meter/article/2016/dec/05/how-pizzagate-went-fake-news-real-problem-dc-busin/

9 www.politifact.com/florida/statements/2014/may/08/blog-posting/florida-democrats-just-voted-impose-sharia-law-wom/

10 Ryan Tate, 'Google CEO: Secrets Are for Filthy People', Gawker Media, 4 Dec. 2009. <http://gawker.com/5419271/google-ceo-secrets-are-for-filthy-people>.

11 Kashmir Hill, 'How Target Figured Out a Teen Girl Was Pregnant Before Her Father Did', *Forbes*, 16 Feb. 2012. <http://www.forbes.com/sites/kashmirhill/2012/02/16/how-target-figured-out-a-teen-girl-was-pregnant-before-her-father-did/#4df94eb134c6>.

# Index

enterprise software 33–5, 47, 72; ERP *see*
Enterprise Resource Planning (ERP)
Epinions.com 216
EQT, Motherbrain xiii, 213–14, 222
Ericsson 167–8
European Union referendum, UK xv, 263–4
Evernote 21
executive/boardroom use of Outside
Insight 125–50, 275–6, 279–80
external data/information xi–xii, 48–62,
81–90; analytic problems 229, 239;
comparison with internal data 229;
correcting insular bias 81–4, 90; and the
Internet of Things 258–61; leading
indicators xii; and NLP viii, 239–41, 242;
OI, decision-making and 72–4 *see also*
decision-making, corporate; online data
as decision-making blind spot 51–2;
real-time *see* real-time analytics/external
data; from satellite imagery 253–8, 260

Facebook 4–5, 12, 15, 66, 77, 105, 166, 177,
183, 268; founding of x; and Instagram
59, 60, 61, 146–7; IPO planning 59;
Messenger xiv, 77, 78; NYPD
monitoring unit xii, 5–7; profiles and
'likes' 246, 265–6, 268; real-time
monitoring by British police 95–6; and the
US presidential elections 156, 157, 265–6;
and VOR 68
fake news 267, 271–2
FedEx 116, 118–19
Fiat Mio 186–7
financial crisis, 2007–2008 83–90
financials, company xvi, 24, 27, 61, 128, 132,
143–4, 146, 147, 277, 278
Finney, Hal 176
Fishman, Steve 88–9
Fitbit 194
Fletcher, Alan 249
Flickr 3, 95, 96
Flight Quest Challenge 105–6
Foldit 191–3
Ford, Henry 112
Fortune 500 companies 39
Fortune 1000 companies 126–7, 238

Friele 73–4
Fuld, Dick 89

Galbo, Mike 243
Galland, Brad 49–50
game theory 130, 147, 279
Gartner 35
Gates, Bill 35
GE Hospital Quest challenge 242–4
General Electric 105–6, 107
Genic.ai 263
GNU project 183
Goldbloom, Anthony 242
Goldman Sachs 12, 82
Google 77, 177, 183, 208; AdWords 20, 103;
Maps 92–3; PageRank 251; Play 58, 59;
and YouTube 109, 146–7
Graney, Russ 243
Greater Manchester Police 95–6
Gregory, Joe 89–90
Gresvig, Knut 168
*Guinness Book of World Records* 151
Gulliver, Stuart 206
Gxav &* 107

Haiti earthquake 92–3
Hamner, Ben 242
Hanno, Dennis 39
Harrison, John 179–80
*Harvard Business Review* 115, 140–41
Hastings, Reed 191
Hazelwood Street 199–202
hedge funds 218–22
Heins, Thorstein 41
Hewlett-Packard (HP) 14–15, 103, 216
Hike Messenger xv, 77–9
Hinton, Geoffrey 191
Horner, Matt 177
Howe, Jeff 180–81
HSBC 206
Hughes, Pat 200

IBM 15, 188–9, 189
Idibon 239–41, 252
Iknowwhereyourcatlives.com 3
Initial Public Offerings (IPOs) 12, 59

# INDEX